WORSHIP FOUNDRY
SHAPING A NEW GENERATION OF WORSHIP LEADERS

JAMIE HARVILL

Leaders — Teams — Volunteers — Students — Congregations

WestBow Press
A DIVISION OF THOMAS NELSON

Copyright © 2013 Jamie Harvill.

All rights reserved. No part of this book may be used or reproduced by any means, graphic, electronic, or mechanical, including photocopying, recording, taping or by any information storage retrieval system without the written permission of the publisher except in the case of brief quotations embodied in critical articles and reviews.

WestBow Press books may be ordered through booksellers or by contacting:

WestBow Press
A Division of Thomas Nelson
1663 Liberty Drive
Bloomington, IN 47403
www.westbowpress.com
1 (866) 928-1240

Because of the dynamic nature of the Internet, any web addresses or links contained in this book may have changed since publication and may no longer be valid. The views expressed in this work are solely those of the author and do not necessarily reflect the views of the publisher, and the publisher hereby disclaims any responsibility for them.

Any people depicted in stock imagery provided by Thinkstock are models, and such images are being used for illustrative purposes only. Certain stock imagery © Thinkstock.

Scriptures taken from the Holy Bible, New International Version®, NIV®. Copyright © 1973, 1978, 1984, 2011 by Biblica, Inc.™ Used by permission of Zondervan. All rights reserved worldwide. www.zondervan.com The "NIV" and "New International Version" are trademarks registered in the United States Patent and Trademark Office by Biblica, Inc.™ All rights reserved.

ISBN: 978-1-4908-0997-7 (sc)
ISBN: 978-1-4908-0998-4 (e)

Library of Congress Control Number: 2013917781

Printed in the United States of America.

WestBow Press rev. date: 10/4/2013

TABLE OF CONTENTS

Introduction.. vii
Acknowledgments... ix

Section 1: Leadership ....**xi**
Chapter 1 – The Worship Leader..1
Chapter 2 – Curator of the Arts...11
Chapter 3 – Leading a Diverse Group of Individuals.........................15
Chapter 4 – What's In a Title?...19

Section 2: Foundations for Worship Ministry **29**
Chapter 5 – Worship and Virtue...31
Chapter 6 – A Worshiping Church 35
Chapter 7 – Technology, Tradition and Change 39
Chapter 8 – So I'm A Worship Leader—Now What? 43

Section 3: Team Building **49**
Chapter 9 – Building a Team around an Organizational Plan..........51
Chapter 10 – The Team Selection Process...57
Chapter 11 – The Tech Team: Confessions of a Church Sound
                Engineer...61
Chapter 12 – The Audition Process...69
Chapter 13 – The Worship Team Agreement..77

Section 4: Planning and Preparation **87**
Chapter 14 – Life Lessons from the Road (My Personal Journey).....89
Chapter 15 – The Concept of "Flow"...93
Chapter 16 – The Ultimate Goal of the Service 99

Chapter 17 – Rehearsal Preparation..103
Chapter 18 – Chord Charts and Lead Sheets...107
Chapter 19 – Planning a Service...115
Chapter 20 – Tips for a Successful Rehearsal.......................................125

Section 5: The Worship Service..**129**
Chapter 21 – Engaging the Congregation 131
Chapter 22 – Stage Zones..139
Chapter 23 – Arranging for Band and Vocals 143
Chapter 24 – The Worship Service Producer...157
Chapter 25 – When a Service Seems Too Slick.......................................159
Chapter 26 – When Things Go Wrong During a Service 165
Chapter 27 – Garments of Praise (Worship Attire) 169

Section 6: Legacy **173**

Resources...181

INTRODUCTION

It was a life-changing decade for me, but by 1979 I was in a quandary as to what to do with my life. A small church in my neighborhood needed a young leader for their youth group. As a 19-year-old, I was only a year or so older than some of the ones I would be leading. I jumped into the job wet behind the ears. Only four years earlier, in the spring of 1975, I made Christ my Lord, and now I was called to step up and be a leader—no longer just a follower.

I soon realized how the pastor of that small church was disrespected and bullied by the very congregation he tried to lead. I made a mental note that I would never find myself in that kind of situation. But all of us who have spent time in ministry have learned that church leadership is in stark contrast to simply being a church member—one of the flock. Unfortunately, the pastor of that small church would continue to be bullied, and his ministry was basically reactionary; he spent most of his time dodging stones that the church counsel would fling at him.

At that early, tender stage in ministry, I had no mentors or anyone to come around and tell me that being on a church staff could be something fulfilling, something that could actually bring joy. By January of 1980 I was invited to leave Fullerton, California—the place where I was raised and home of that little neighborhood church—to tour the world as a professional musician. I put ministry on hold for a time. After all, who would want to invest their life in ministry when the very people you serve become the enemy? Regrettably, many ministers have come to ride out their careers just like the pastor of my first church: hunkered-down in a defensive position. Could ministry be fun? Could there be a place in a church for a musician like me? Could I become a full-time minister and encourage others to be the same?

A year earlier, during the fall semester of 1978, I asked one of my professors at Golden West College—who was also a Christian and a music professional—if he thought I should become a secular musician or a Christian musician. He seemed amused at first, but said that *I'd have to figure that out on my own*. It seems as though I've been figuring things out on my own ever since. I must say that the Lord has guided me through it all, but in the ensuing thirty-plus years since those early days, I have come to realize that not much has changed in the Church. I feel it's about time we seriously mentor young people, to help guide them, to help form them into effective ministers—way before they enter college and before they go on to seminary. I eventually returned to ministry, but what I would learn in college wouldn't be near enough to prepare me for the real-world of working on a church staff and leading people.

We have an incredible opportunity to raise up dynamic, Spirit-filled, well-equipped, powerhouse ministers to take the Gospel into the 21st century. Great musicians and ministers are in demand, but we have done a poor job of putting especially those with a high-degree of musical talent onto our church stages without first giving them a solid foundation in leadership, ministry team building, theological, musical and technical training, and proper time for their own spiritual formation. In short, I feel that many of the young worship leaders of our era are fatherless; they have been put out there in ministry because they are good guitar players, singers, performers, artists, or whatever. They've been given a platform without proper oversight, support and training. The results can be damaging to the individuals and to the churches they serve.

This book, *Worship Foundry*, is a self-contained mentorship program. Its pages encompass just about everything I would want a student of worship to know—the most important items that I feel a successful worship leader must have in their toolbox. If there was a desert island list of things I would leave with someone, these pages contain the nuggets that I feel will get them started on the path to success.

A foundry is a factory that produces metal castings. *Worship Foundry* is not a factory, but rather a course through which worship leaders, ministers and musicians of all ages can be shaped, formed by the hand of God, purified with fire, and made into vessels for the Holy Spirit to use in a world that sorely needs Jesus.

ACKNOWLEDGMENTS

A big "thank you" goes out to my beautiful bride of almost thirty years, Brenda. She has patiently edited my writing, and I'm sure she wanted to pull her hair out many times! Thanks to my son, Josh, for bringing his graphic art skills to this book; to my daughter, Betsy, for being my biggest fan and encourager; to my late mother, Betty, who gave me the gift of music; and to my dad, Tom, from whom I inherited the gift of the written word.

I now lay this book in the hands of my Savior and Lord as a sacrifice of praise for the life and the blessings He's bestowed upon me, His servant. May these words stir the flame in every reader's heart to share the hope of Christ as a leader and worshiper. My biggest request from those who read these pages is that they become a mentor to someone—one's legacy will be remembered through the love, care, teaching, prayer and encouragement deposited in the hearts of hungry souls, long after the giver is gone.

Jamie Harvill
Spring Hill, Tennessee
August, 2013

SECTION 1:
LEADERSHIP

THE WORSHIP LEADER

Smelly Fish

I've often heard the old expression, "A fish stinks from the head down!" I know it's a rather abrupt way to start a book and the first chapter on character as it applies to a worship leader. But "leader" is a part of the job description. Whether we like it or not, our behavior in relation to both God and others will help determine the success or failure of our worship leadership.

Some may think that a worship leader or church music director (whatever the title) is a non-ministry position. Those who are currently serving in a worship ministry—be it as an arranger, instrumentalist, singer or even an administrator—may not feel that they signed-up for the ministry part, perhaps because they are not ordained or theologically trained. But if one accepts the position of music director or worship leader in church ministry, Godly character, behavior and integrity are essential components to the job—along with a measure of musical, technical and administrative skills. Even though we may not serve in the pastoral division of our church staff, as Christians we are certainly *all* ministers.

The way we conduct our daily affairs outside of the church building, our relationship with others on staff and the volunteer teams, our position in the greater community, and especially the way we treat people in general, will set the tone for those who follow us. Our worship ministries look like us. If we are full of the Spirit, and act accordingly, then it's probably a good chance that our ministry reflects that. Like the "smelly fish" heading suggests, when problems pop up and there's a "foul odor" in the ministry, it starts with the head honcho: the leader. The leader may not have been directly responsible for the problems at hand, but ultimately it's the leader who'll have to deal with the "odor."

The Christ-Follower

It may seem presumptuous to think that all church staff members or lay leaders are Christ-followers. Sadly, I've personally witnessed that so-called "ministers" can function on a church staff without a personal commitment to Christ.

I know of one friend who had a successful recording career and then went on to take a worship ministry position in a church. During an evangelistic service, he realized he had never before asked Christ to be his Lord and Savior. It took a great amount of courage to walk forward and shake the hand of the preacher that night, especially when my friend was the worship director, leading songs from the same pulpit from which the convicting message was preached. My friend humbly made the decision, in front of his colleagues and congregation, to follow Christ. What a difference that decision made in his subsequent ministry! Having a personal and intimate relationship with Jesus Christ—the focus of our praise, adoration and worship—is step-one in the journey of any worship leader.

In any other capacity, simply musical, technical, and administrative skills may suffice. But as a worship leader, we are representing the very God of the universe to a lost world. Our churches look to us for encouragement from on and off the stage, on a daily and weekly basis. Whether or not you signed-up for the job, you represent the Kingdom and the Church. Your relationship with the Savior is at the heart of your effectiveness as a worship leader.

Leadership is Influence

One's personal character is an essential component of leadership. In the book, *The 21 Irrefutable Laws of Leadership*, John Maxwell sums up his definition of leadership: "Leadership is influence—nothing more, nothing less."

Not every appointed leader has followers. Sometimes the "boss" has little or no influence on other people. A subordinate may in fact hold more credibility than the specified leader. Therefore, the second in command may very well be the true "boss."

Giving attention, respect, and honor to those on our team encourages them to follow us. A positive influence starts with our concern for others. It's when we try and force our authority upon people that we show a lack of true leadership. When the fruit of the Spirit is alive and growing in our lives, we are inclined to respond to the needs of others, as Christ does the Church. Sometimes we are called to make courageous and possibly unpopular decisions as a leader. Our character helps those who follow us to trust that we are moving in the right direction, even when they are uncertain about the road we choose to get there. As humans we sometimes fail. Being the first to admit that we made a mistake sheds light on our true motivation.

We must also understand that influence doesn't always come through virtuous deeds. The renowned Peter Drucker—writer, professor, management consultant and self-described "social ecologist," who explored the way human beings organize themselves—sums up leadership as: "... someone who has followers." We know that many world leaders have risen to power through dishonorable means. So the term *leader,* according to Drucker, doesn't always connote a positive role model. Just look at some politicians and dictators who force their way upon the world stage through oppression, mayhem and murder (They usually perish by the same method).

Living Life with Purpose

Warren Bennis is an American scholar, organizational consultant and author. He is widely regarded as the pioneer of the contemporary field of leadership. His focuses much more on the individual capability of a leader: "Leadership," he says, "is a function of knowing yourself, having a vision that is well communicated, building trust among colleagues, and taking effective action to realize your own leadership potential."

When we study the life of Jesus using the Bennis definition of leadership, we see that:

1. **Jesus knew He was the Son of God** (Matthew 26:64).

2. **Jesus knew and effectively communicated His purpose** (He came to seek and save the lost: [Luke 19:10]; to be King and a witness to

the Truth [John 18:37], and a light in the world [John 12:46]; to die on the cross [John 12:27]; to be the Savior of the world [John 3:16-18]).

3. **Jesus was a skilled leader** (Mobilized Seventy [Luke 1-:1-12; 18-20]; Trained Twelve: [Mark 3:14-19; 1 Thessalonians. 2:8, John 14:12-14]; Confided in Three: [Matthew 17:1-3, Mark 9:2-3, Mark 14:33-34, Luke 9:28, Mark 5:37-43] from "The Leadership Strategy of Jesus," by Michael Hyatt).

4. **Jesus lived up to His full potential and fulfilled His calling** (Jesus turned the world upside down: Acts 17:6).

Using Mr. Bennis' definition of leadership, here are some strategies for us to follow:

1. Get to know yourself

When someone asks another person who they are, in jest my dad often says: "Look at your driver's license!" I wish it were that simple. Many know very little about their family background. It may be the result of being adopted or the failure of parents to share their heritage—perhaps due to embarrassment, or the simple lack of available historical information. But without knowing vital information about ourselves, we may lose the motivation to move forward.

Getting to know one's self can be a bit tricky since our outlook on life is inextricably tied to how we were raised and our individual personalities. Some reading this may have experienced a difficult childhood. Some, on the other hand, may have experienced unconditional love and acceptance. Many, like me, did not grow up in a Christian household. My own conversion to Christianity happened when I was fourteen-years-old, during high school. It was only after my life-changing decision that my parents themselves received Christ. After that, our home took on a whole new dynamic.

What I have become today, though, isn't limited by my family heritage, ethnic background, culture or past. As a Christ-follower, I have been bought and freed from slavery to sin through the blood of Jesus. My response to God's forgiveness has opened up new opportunities to collaborate with the Creator, and I am motivated by hope for the future.

Worship Foundry

The ability to cooperate with God through faith may bring challenges. Our difficulties may be the result of a chemical imbalance, an emotional challenge, a physical limitation, or a combination of all, but we can know that the foundation of our life is anchored in Christ, and the strength to do great things in the Kingdom and for others is available through *His* power—with *His* resources!

In 2 Corinthians 5:17, Paul states: "Therefore, if anyone is in Christ, the new creation has come: The old has gone, the new is here!" The discovery of *who I am* today is based on my *new life in Christ. Our limitations are not deal-breakers to God!*

2. Discover a *vision* for your future

My friend Dr. John Stanko has spent most of his career talking with others and teaching about finding one's life purpose. He has a passion for purpose, and when you attend one of his seminars or read his blog, you can't help but get on the road to discover your own life-purpose.

Dr. Stanko teaches from the standpoint that every person has a life-purpose; that everyone has the potential to discover their purpose, learn to define it, articulate it, and make life-choices through the filter of that purpose. Before we become true leaders, we must have the ability to state our vision for the future in a clear way that motivates others to walk with us toward that goal. If we are apprehensive or uncertain, others will be, too. It's never too early—or too late—to begin discovering your purpose, to look into your life for the seeds of purpose that God planted in you before you were born.

Through his ministry, *Purpose Quest*, Dr. Stanko answers the question: *What should I do once my purpose is found?* Stanko responds, "It may sound strange...but you don't have to do anything. God wants you to fulfill your purpose more than you do, so He will meet you more than half way. The fulfillment of purpose will find you. That doesn't mean you don't have to get ready and improve. Take lessons, read books, practice, go to places where your purpose is celebrated, but don't feel like you have to do something. Rest in God and watch Him bring the problems to you for which you are the solution."

Dr. Stanko goes on to say, "It's all about doing what you love doing. Why would God give you a love to do something—and God has created you and is intimately acquainted with all your ways—and then not allow you to

Jamie Harvill

do it? Is God a tease? He is not! So find what gives you joy and do it as often as possible. If people pay you to do it, fine. If not, then do it when the kids are in bed or after your paying job. Don't try to figure it out or rationalize it, just do it and let God lead you where you need to be, where you want to be—to a place where the joy of the Lord is your strength."

Without exploring the detailed steps here, one can learn more about purpose by taking advantage of the *Purpose Quest* website and its many resources (www.purposequest.com).

3. Maintain a Good Reputation

When I started the sixth grade, I learned that my reputation preceded me—or, should I say, my brother's reputation did! As I settled into my sixth-grade school year, the teacher seemed immediately distant, and her obvious irritation caused me to feel insecure. After sharing about the "mean" new teacher, my mother knew the problem was more about my brother than me. Let me explain.

My older brother stormed through that frustrated teacher's sixth-grade class like a tornado four years earlier. His strident behavior was magnified by hyperactivity. He was prescribed medication for this problem, but it never seemed to calm him. Apparently he was the talk of the teacher's lounge way before I even entered kindergarten. I was automatically labeled a "hooligan" by my new sixth-grade teacher—which was my supposed fate. Being Robbie's brother, in her mind, meant I was going to be just like him.

The truth is, I was nothing like my older brother: I was fairly quiet, compliant, and a decent student. Was it fair that I was judged by the standard my brother helped create? Certainly not—but it does say something about reputation and its huge impact on one's future! Thankfully, my mother rescued me from that sixth-grade teacher and moved me to another school, where I eventually thrived and earned a good reputation of my own!

Consistency = Trust

Building trust with others requires consistency. If I say one thing and do another, people will have a hard time trusting me. It really isn't what we *say* that counts as much as what we consistently *do* that builds trust in relationships, teams and organizations. Unfortunately, some people use their pre-conceived notions about us to make initial judgments.

For instance, have you ever met someone, or seen them from a distance, and they reminded you of someone else in the past who may have done you wrong? Somehow their behavior is much like the person who hurt you, or their appearance favors them in some way. We protect ourselves from being hurt again by becoming defensive. Unfortunately, each of us will make hasty judgments based on emotion and not fact from time to time.

Be Who You Say You Are

Our opinions about people are better served through what Sgt. Friday from the old television show "Dragnet" would say to talkative witnesses: "Just stick to the facts, please!" The point is: We must make an effort as leaders to "be" who we *say* we "are." In fact, leaders are held to a higher standard. In Hebrews 13:7-8 it says: "Remember your leaders, who spoke the word of God to you. Consider the outcome of their way of life and imitate their faith. Jesus Christ is the same yesterday and today and forever."

In Christian music, I have seen many performers portray one thing to the public, but live a life incongruous to those beliefs in private. I learned years ago as I traveled the world as a musician, clinician and minister, that there are as many theological points of view as there are Christians. With so many differing opinions, rules, beliefs and viewpoints in Christianity, one can go crazy trying to please everyone.

So, as leaders we must be wise. The Apostle Paul wrote in 1 Corinthians 10:23: "All things are lawful, but not all things are profitable. All things are lawful, but not all things edify." Sometimes we need to say "no" to things with which we have personal freedom in order to prevent others from stumbling in their faith. In the big picture, though, our greatest allegiance should be to God; no human system of theology will be our judge when we're called to give an account before the Almighty on Judgment Day!

It's important to remember that we are constantly being scrutinized, so we must make wise choices as we serve in our churches and communities. Our reputations are of utmost importance to our future as ministers, even as musicians and worship leaders. We lead the congregation each week, usually from the same spot on the stage where the sermon is delivered. Therefore, we must live to bring honor and glory to God.

Jamie Harvill

4. Learn to Become an Effective Leader

Some may say, "Leaders are born not made." I think that we all have potential in leadership because most people are called to lead in some fashion—whether as a parent, an older sibling, in a marriage, or even as a co-worker. As mentioned earlier, not every "stated leader" has followers. Our positive influence on others has a bearing on who will follow us. We can learn to be more effective leaders, and this has much to do with how we prepare for the task of leading. I believe a true leader gets way out ahead of the pack through careful thought, preparation, finding the bumps in the road, problem solving, and counting the cost of getting to a destination. I ask every conceivable question about a task or an event.

To illustrate, here's how I initiate basic event planning as an example of leadership. In the planning stage, I use a yellow pad and write at the top of the page the name and the purpose of the event. Then I jot down times, locations, people and an order of activities. I also make a sketch of the physical set up and make notes about needed resources. With all of the details listed on the page in front of me, I can see the full scale of the event. A timeline is so very important to establish so all of the planning, preparation, promotion and implementation has sufficient time to be rolled out.

I begin with the event itself and work backward to the starting point of planning. That way I can determine how much total time is involved before setting the schedule and notifying the participants. I will also include self-imposed deadlines for every process on the to-do list. If a budget has already been designated for an event I make sure the expenses are commensurate.

I look at all the potential problems that could happen with an event—take for example a worship service. I always make sure the stage is set properly before rehearsal and the service. I make sure, along with our tech team, that all of the instrument cables are in place. I make sure that there are extra music charts available for the band and singers in case someone forgets to bring their own. I have a guitar string changing kit at the side of the stage in case a guitarist or bass player breaks a string during the service. I have several extra microphone and instrument cables, power cords and strips, and various battery sizes on hand, just in case of failure. I ask a million questions to myself and do my very best to be ready for any potential problems that may arise. I can never be over-prepared!

Worship Foundry

$\bullet \quad \bullet \quad \bullet$

Leading Volunteers

With most church activities the work is done through volunteers—people who have families, jobs, and many responsibilities in their personal lives. I highly respect the time given by volunteers for events, rehearsals, worship services, community outreaches, building projects, etc., and that's why I start and end on time.

The best currency for volunteers is appreciation. It's important to convey appreciation during and after each event. It's also good to have "hi-five" moments when an event goes over well, and equally important to make necessary corrections, with love, when something doesn't go as well. Volunteers want to be a part of something exciting, life-changing, and carried out with excellence and efficiency. As a leader, it's my responsibility to bring direction and discipline to the whole process. Volunteers want to feel *respected, protected* and *appreciated.*

Becoming an effective leader is a life-long process, and it's important to invest in leadership, as well as spiritual and musical training. This book will speak of leadership throughout, but there are so many resources available in Christian bookstores. Books by contemporary authors such as John Maxwell and Bill Hybels, and even classics like "D.L. Moody on Spiritual Leadership" are available in print or in e-book form. There are seminars such as the annual *Willow Creek Leadership Summit,* simulcast from the Chicago-area main campus to local churches throughout the world. Training videos are available on the *Willow Creek* website to help you become a more effective leader.

It's not too late to finish your college or graduate degree. There are many universities that offer online courses on leadership. The opportunity to complete what you may have started years ago can be invigorating. Any investment that makes us a better person, leader, minister, and musician is a good one.

Jesus' Method of Leadership

Jesus made sure the disciples knew that the true essence of leadership was *being a servant.* He taught them through the humble task of washing the

Jamie Harvill

disciples' feet. Even though some relented, Jesus pressed-in to make His point. In John 13:12-16, we see Jesus, the ultimate servant, in action:

"When he had finished washing their feet, he put on his clothes and returned to his place. 'Do you understand what I have done for you?' he asked them. 'You call me 'Teacher' and 'Lord,' and rightly so, for that is what I am. Now that I, your Lord and Teacher, have washed your feet, you also should wash one another's feet. I have set you an example that you should do as I have done for you. Very truly I tell you, no servant is greater than his master, nor is a messenger greater than the one who sent him. Now that you know these things, you will be blessed if you do them.'"

There is no greater display of true leadership than in the life Jesus. His way of dealing with people, prioritizing His time (He did what He was called to do in roughly three years), and making courageous and unpopular decisions, is a great example of true focus, passion and purpose. His obedience to God is our example to emulate. His behavior inspires us to get up, get out and be the leader we need to be. Our understanding of people, human nature, and how to inspire a diverse team of individuals, with a focused goal, is imperative to effective leadership.

CURATOR OF THE ARTS

Curator- from Latin: one who cares, from *cūrāre* to care for something

On leadership and creativity: "There are two ways of being creative: One can sing and dance. Or one can create an environment in which singers and dancers flourish."— Warren Bennis

The greatest example of ingenuity (the quality of being clever, original, and inventive) is God. In Genesis 1:27, we see that God created mankind in His own image. Two things are in effect here: 1) God is creative, making us in His own image and, therefore, 2) we are also creative beings.

Before God made the world and populated it, He imagined it, and then went on to create what He had in his mind.

God's ingenuity differs from human creativity, and it is summarized in the Latin phrase, *"creatio ex nihilo,"* which simply means: *God creates things out of nothing.* In other words, God didn't require wood, steel, stone or clay to create the world and its inhabitants. He imagined the earth—the elements, plants, animals and human beings—and out of the void, at His command, they appeared.

Jamie Harvill

Out of the Soil

It's interesting that God chose to form mankind out of soil from the ground. One of God's purposes was for mankind to create a livelihood from the earth, and He knew that human survival would depend upon creativity, and the ability to construct tools and solve complex problems through ingenuity.

Genesis chapter 1, in *The Good News Translation*, gives very specific purposes for which the male and female were created. In verses 26-31, we read:

> *"Then God said, 'And now we will make human beings; they will be like us and resemble us. They will have power over the fish, the birds, and all animals, domestic and wild, large and small.' So God created human beings, making them to be like himself. He created them male and female, blessed them, and said, 'Have many children, so that your descendants will live all over the earth and bring it under their control. I am putting you in charge of the fish, the birds, and all the wild animals. I have provided all kinds of grain and all kinds of fruit for you to eat; but for all the wild animals and for all the birds I have provided grass and leafy plants for food'—and it was done. God looked at everything he had made, and he was very pleased. Evening passed and morning came—that was the sixth day."*

The long and short of it is: *God made humans to be creative: we were given resources to create, and the ability to care for and cultivate all that fills the earth.*

Beautifully Made

God crafted a splendid work of art when He made the galaxy; His handiwork is seen in all of creation, and His workmanship is perfect and full of beauty.

In Romans 1:20, Paul argues that the existence of God is evident, "For since the creation of the world God's invisible qualities—his eternal power and divine nature—have been clearly seen, being understood from what has been made, so that people are without excuse."

Worship Foundry

Every human being innately recognizes *beauty* (that which pleasurably exalts the mind or spirit). God has placed the concept of *beauty* in the human heart. Therefore, when we see something "beautiful," it resonates in our soul.

Eye of the Beholder

Dr. Matthew R. Schulman, MD, assistant professor of plastic surgery at The Mount Sinai School of Medicine in New York, recently published an article about beauty as it relates to the human face. In it he says:

"Our quest for beauty isn't a modern obsession. Philosophers and poets chronicle the importance of beauty—and the virtues that accompany it. In *Timaeus*, Plato states that 'The good, of course, is always beautiful.' *In Ode on a Grecian Urn*, Keats writes that 'Beauty is truth, truth beauty—that is all.' And Emerson describes beauty as 'The mark God sets upon virtue.'"

Dr. Schulman goes on to describe characteristics of beauty, two of which are *symmetry* and *proportion*. The *Merriam Webster Dictionary* defines symmetry as "beauty of form arising from balanced proportions."

With this in mind, God speaks to the heart of man, and reaches deep into his soul through music, the visual arts, the dramatic arts and literature. God uses the medium of art, through the Holy Spirit, to reveal Himself to us.

Like Plato, Keats and Emerson, we see *goodness, truth* and *virtue* in beauty. This is why the arts are so vital in communicating the Gospel to the church and to a lost world.

The Arts and the Church

From the beginning, the early church used the arts to communicate the Gospel. The evidence is seen in:

- Frescos painted on the walls of early church buildings with Christian symbols and scenes from the Bible
- The use of songs, hymns and spiritual songs in worship (Ephesians 5:19)
- Beautiful colored glass windows that were introduced to the English Isle by St. Benedict Biscop (628-690), who initiated a great program in architecture and art

Jamie Harvill

- Dramas, known as "miracle plays," that were implemented in English-speaking churches as early as 1110, and were encouraged by the priests to give religious instruction to the people
- Iconography, in the form painting and sculpture, depicting religious figures, was important to the early Church
- Dance in a worship setting is mentioned numerous times throughout the Old Testament. Because the word *dance* appears only a few times in the New Testament, many would argue that it is not appropriate for the Church today. I differ in that view, based on the beautiful parable of the Prodigal Son (Luke 15:24-25), and the wonderful teaching on celebration by Jesus Himself. Because the son returned, the father declared a party in his honor. The passage describes that during the celebration, the Father's house was filled with "music and dancing." I believe that dancing, just as with all of the arts, when done with reverence, is a beautiful way of displaying praise to God! Dr. Ann Stevenson, in her book, *Dance! [God's Holy Purpose]*, with reference to the Prodigal story, wrote, "This dancing in the Father's house was due to the salvation of his child. We must rejoice in the God of our salvation. Salvation is the foundational reason for our dance."

The Role of *Curator* in the Church

The arts are thriving in the Church today—in some churches more than others. It's important that worship leaders consider themselves *those who care for the arts in the local church*. A curator is one who *manages* and *oversees* the ministry of worship—extending from music to all forms of artistic expression.

Sometimes a worship leader is hired as the sole artistic/creative force on the church staff. In other cases, the senior pastor or another staff member joins with the worship leader to develop the use of the arts in communicating the Gospel. Working with others requires cooperation between members of the church staff, and with differing viewpoints and personality types, conflict is inevitable.

LEADING A DIVERSE GROUP OF INDIVIDUALS

Each person is born with a unique set of abilities. Successful businesses and effective ministry teams are purposely constructed to incorporate diverse talents. A good leader is wise to enlist talented people who together complete necessary tasks and, with excellence, meet the challenges at hand. There is a tendency for some leaders to hire people similar to themselves, and this will eventually bring weakness to an organization.

In the case of Abraham Lincoln, when he was challenged to build his cabinet of advisors following the election of 1860, he chose a diverse team of rivals to help lead the nation through one of its darkest periods.

Whichever personality trait we possess, as worship leaders we have the task of working with all types of people in ministry—musicians, singers, technical people, pastors, artists and administrators—some who prefer to work alone, and others who thrive on a team. Some members will try to do as little work as possible, while others, in the extreme, will over-analyze and belabor the tasks at hand.

The greatest of leaders bring team members together with varying strengths that compliment weaknesses. If everyone on the team has the same skill-set, then very little would be accomplished at the end of the day. To bring order to a worship ministry, and to do what needs to be done on a weekly basis, it takes a wide variety of skills and personalities.

Jamie Harvill

The Creative Personality: Not Crazy, Just Eccentric

Every team is strengthened when including creative persons. In the case of a music ministry, there are usually more creative types involved than others. An effective team, to an outsider, may look like Lincoln's team of rivals, and it probably should! Creative people, administrative people, technical people—all with a heart and goal of ministry—are those of which a successful ministry team is comprised.

Some creative people are so imaginative that their behavior—the way they dress and the way they relate to others—may seem eccentric. Their manner may have a tendency to irritate the more administrative-type personalities on the team. We all know someone who is exceptionally creative, and if you can't think of one, maybe you're that village creative-type yourself!

A common mistake is to dismiss creativity as frivolous. I've seen leaders, with high measures of administrative skills, attempt to make a creative person into an administrator, accountant or technician. This usually leads to disaster. Trying to force an administrative-type person into a creative mold can result in failure as well.

Many creative personalities have the poor reputation of being disorganized, late to meetings, lazy, etc. This may apply to some, but creative people are quite methodical when it comes to their work. Because what they accomplish seems so effortless, others may not recognize the process as being sophisticated. As in all successful teams, complimentary skill-sets create balance in an organization.

The Administrator: Order Out of Chaos

My friend Dr. John Stanko has shared that one of his greatest purposes on earth is to bring *order out of chaos*. The calling of a leader is to bring organization to any endeavor. It's important that creative types, who are also leaders, learn organization skills, or bring others onto the team to help accomplish order.

Administrative types get a bad rap, too. To creative-types it seems admin-types are all about details, numbers and schedules. To a great extent, that's how their brain is wired. But without administrators we wouldn't have the organization necessary to operate efficiently. We wouldn't have a driving

Worship Foundry

force behind budgets, schedules, and maintaining the infrastructure of the organization as it applies to buildings, maintenance, and getting people physically from one place to another.

Emotional vs. Cognitive

Without getting into incredibly complex theories of human behavior, people respond to their surroundings in both emotional and cognitive ways. It is also found that people function, to a higher degree, within one or the other sphere. I'm not trying to oversimplify, because every person operates out of a very intricate, interwoven series of intellectual and emotional impulses in the brain. It's just that some people tend to look at life through a cognitive (thinking-oriented) lens, and others primarily through an emotional (feelings-oriented) one. This is not at all to suggest that organized people aren't in touch with their feelings, or that creative people aren't intelligent! Rather, it's good to understand personality traits so that we can better communicate as a team.

To illuminate the contrast between the creative thought process and that of an average person, writer Jeffrey Paul Baumgartner, in article from *The Creativity Post*, observes: "Creative people make more use of their mental raw material and practice less intellectual regulation." He explains: "When you give an average person a creative challenge, she tends immediately to try and come up with ideas. But because her mind is too focused on the issues of the challenge, her ideas are limited in scope as well. They are conventional, obvious ideas. The highly creative person, on the other hand, tends to turn the problem around in her head. She asks questions, thinks about it in various scenarios and brings seemingly unrelated information into her problem solving."

Baumgartner goes on to describe the concept of *intellectual regulation*. He explains that: "[it] includes the brain's censorship bureau: the bit of the brain that prevents us from saying or doing inappropriate things. It allows us to control impulses and to choose appropriate courses of behavior according to our circumstances. It seems that in highly creative people, this part of the brain becomes much less active during times of creation. This makes sense. If you can reduce the level of thought regulation when generating creative work (whether ideas, music, or artwork), then fewer ideas will be filtered out as inappropriate and more will be developed and shared."

Jamie Harvill

I ran across another interesting perspective on administrative people from author Gene C. Fant, Jr., in an article from the *Chronicle of Higher Education,* titled "Micromanagers and Administrative Types." He points out the common perceptions people have of the classic manager-type. It seems he is taking a shot at administrators, but the author is actually a university department chair and an administrator himself. He writes:

"I've told the stories of my two favorite micromanaging supervisors, one who used to patrol the hallways with a pad and pen trying to catch folks who had missed office hours even for five-minutes, and one who used to squat outside of classrooms with his right ear pressed to the door. I can't think about either of them without giggling at their silliness."

Fant defines a *good administrator*: "Good administrators look for ways to *create efficiencies that matter.* I highly recommend that search committees ponder that observation as they examine applicants for positions, especially for department-chair positions."

5 Steps to Better Communication

- **Understand your audience**—Consider the personality of each member of the team, and communicate with purpose. Make an effort to talk less, listen more, stay focused, and use humor or a light touch whenever possible
- **Listen with your ears, eyes and body language**—Folded arms, lack of eye contact, a slouching posture, all convey disinterest, contempt and/or defensiveness. Listen and respond with positive and affirming gestures
- **Try to control emotions, especially with "hot topics"**—Be willing and ready to back down from an argument. Being "right" as a leader doesn't necessarily move the team forward
- **Lay out expectations clearly**—Keep promises; be fair when discipline is required; reward victories
- **Communicate often**—Avoid the *"I told you I loved you when I married you"* style of communication. Caring for the team through emails, memos, social media, birthday cards, and thank you notes can all be effective ways to maintain a leader's influence

WHAT'S IN A TITLE?

The term "worship leader" isn't found anywhere in the Bible. In 1Timothy 2:5, Paul states that there is no "mediator" between God and man but Jesus. Therefore, many instances in the Bible where worship takes place, it happens without a specific leader (although in the case of worship in the Tabernacle and the Temple at Jerusalem, there was an organized system and a priesthood to attend to the process of worship). Still, even in the New Testament, as well as in today's churches, God doesn't *require* a worship leader to stand up with an acoustic guitar and a handful of worship choruses to foster worship among His people.

In Hebrews 10:19-22 Paul encourages us to draw near to God:

> *"Therefore, brothers and sisters, since we have confidence to enter the Most Holy Place by the blood of Jesus, by a new and living way opened for us through the curtain, that is, his body, and since we have a great priest over the house of God, let us draw near to God with a sincere heart and with the full assurance that faith brings, having our hearts sprinkled to cleanse us from a guilty conscience and having our bodies washed with pure water."*

In the Old Testament, there was a High Priest who went before God on our behalf (Leviticus 16). Rituals were practiced, including animal sacrifices, and blood was offered to cleanse sin. These annual offerings

Jamie Harvill

on the Day of Atonement were but a precursor, a symbol of what Jesus would eventually accomplish in His death and resurrection. In the New Testament, our new High Priest, Jesus, became the sole sacrifice for our sin, once and for all time. Because of this we now have the confidence to meet and fellowship with God. We, therefore, are encouraged to draw near to God, having been cleansed, with a guilt-free conscience.

Back To the Basics

Jesus is the true *Worship Leader*! We as music ministers are simply servants in our churches, available to help facilitate corporate worship. This music leadership role has rapidly evolved in recent years as the Church strives to remain culturally relevant and to keep up with ever-changing technologies. While improving our corporate worship experiences, we also have an obligation to assist our congregation in their private worship time. As my wife Brenda says: "Often, one's personal worship time is less a priority than their corporate worship; it should be just the opposite!" The songs we sing each week can be excellent tools for spiritual growth, for spreading hope and encouragement.

In Ephesians 5:18-20 we read:

> *"Do not get drunk on wine, which leads to debauchery. Instead, be filled with the Spirit, speaking to one another with psalms, hymns, and songs from the Spirit. Sing and make music from your heart to the Lord, always giving thanks to God the Father for everything, in the name of our Lord Jesus Christ."*

In Hebrews 10:25, Paul writes:

> *"Let us not give up meeting together, as some are in the habit of doing, but let us encourage one another—and all the more as you see the Day approaching."*

<u>As we have seen, God require believers to:</u>

- **Draw near to Him**
- **Be filled with the Holy Spirit**

Worship Foundry

- Speak to one another with psalms, hymns, and songs from the Spirit
- Give thanks to God the Father for everything
- Meet regularly to encourage each other in the faith

Back To the Heart of Worship

What have we created in today's modern version of corporate worship? If in our churches we have strayed from the central focus of Christ, we must find our way back to the heart and soul of worship as it was originally intended.

In the big picture, a worship leader is not just a lead singer: he/she is a shepherd, a minister—one who serves God among people, who creates a team of worshipers to accompany the congregation in worship. Our place in the church is subordinate to the pastor, who ideally is the lead worshiper in the congregation. We serve as an *extension* of the pastor's ministry, and a big part of that is to help instruct and encourage the congregation toward maturity in Christ.

Ever-Changing Tools of the Trade

Every craftsman has a toolbox. A mechanic, a wood worker and a metal fabricator all use tools to help manufacture and maintain their wares. Even in an interpersonal sense, we need skills to communicate and operate in society. Being an effective worship leader requires specific skills and tools, many of which have changed drastically in the past several years.

A degree from seminary or Bible school, with a concentration in choral music and a foundation in classical theory, doesn't fully prepare the 21st century worship leader as it may have in the past. Skills in areas such as team building, leading a worship band and singers while playing guitar or piano, instrumental arranging, knowledge in lighting, sound and video equipment, and proficiency in certain software programs for music notation, audio recording and video editing—all contribute to the success of a contemporary music minister.

Jamie Harvill

A Modern Version of Corporate Worship

Actually, the job description of a worship leader in many large churches today looks much like that of a TV or live concert producer: The pressure to put on a full-blown music and preaching extravaganza each week—incorporating theater lighting and sound, captured on multiple high-definition cameras—can be typical fare.

I've heard it said, "The problem with church is that it happens every week!" The fact is, once we complete last week's production critique, there is barely enough time left to *high-five* our team members because it's necessary to focus on next week's production. Then there's Easter, Christmas and a smattering of special services throughout the calendar year that require our attention.

Look over the requirements for some worship leader positions and you may see a list of qualifying attributes that only Superman could fill! I've even seen smaller churches—200 in attendance or less—looking for super-heroes to fill their worship leader position. Usually, the salary isn't commensurate with the requirements. Some churches like to add student ministries to the load of a worship leader, and when that's required, burnout is a big possibility.

Modern corporate worship—by general definition, and across denominational lines—usually involves a comfortable environment in a clean facility with superb childcare, offering an inspiring time of worship and a spiritually-uplifting message through an excellent audio/visual system, in the span of between one-hour and an hour-and-a-half. The worship experience in the 21st century seems to have evolved into a consumer-oriented activity and the contrast between first-century worship and today is dramatic.

What's A Worship Leader To Do?

When one attempts to break down the job description of a modern effective worship leader, it's a difficult task. With much thought, I will share nine essential traits of a worship leader from an historical point of view—one that doesn't necessarily take into consideration a building, cultural trends, technical aspects, congregation size, denomination or musical style. These traits must serve as goals as we lead our congregations:

Trait 1: Serves the local church with excellence

Charles Dickens, in the classic novel *David Copperfield*, wrote, "My meaning simply is, that whatever I have tried to do in life, I have tried with all my heart to do well; that whatever I have devoted myself to, I have devoted myself to completely; that in great aims and in small, I have always been thoroughly in earnest."

The Free Dictionary defines the adjective *earnest* as: "*With a purposeful or sincere intent; serious; determined.*" As believers, we must *earnestly* give our best, not our leftovers to God. In Colossians 3:17, the Bible says, "And whatever you do, whether in word or deed, do it all in the name of the Lord Jesus, giving thanks to God the Father through him."

As professionals, we pursue excellence. Coach Pat Riley once said, "Excellence is the gradual result of always striving to do better." Not only do we strive for excellence as a *personal standard*, but it shows honor and respect toward our *congregation* and *most importantly, God.*

Trait 2: Is a servant leader

Jesus is a true example of servant-leadership. Through His example we learn how to love, encourage, correct, cast vision, pray, focus and obey God, among many other qualities. Jesus never asked a disciple to go anywhere He wouldn't go Himself.

Ultimately, Jesus was willing to go to the cross on our behalf. He endured physical pain and suffering, rejection, loneliness, and taunting from his executioners and fellow prisoners alike. He went so far as to die for us. Therefore, with Christ's example, we must not only lead others, but serve them, even if it costs us greatly.

Sometimes leaders must ask others to do tough, challenging things. But we must also be willing to make personal sacrifices as servant-leaders— sometimes to the point of suffering. Stephen Covey said it well: "What you do has far greater impact than what you say."

Trait 3: Follows the direction of the Holy Spirit

I've made many mistakes in my life and career by doing things without first asking the Lord; I operated on impulse rather than trusting in God. In

Jamie Harvill

doing so, I usually missed the "best" that He had for me. Thank the Lord that, by His grace, I eventually got back on track!

The direction of the Lord can be found in His *Word*, through *prayer*, and with the *wise counsel* of Godly people. When God asks us to change our plans, then we must follow His lead. If the prompting of the Holy Spirit leads us to make changes in a worship service, do it! God will move in incredible ways when we are sensitive and obedient.

Trait 4: Helps Christ-followers encounter God personally

As worship leaders, it's easy to think of our job as only serving the congregation in larger group settings. But we are also helping individuals draw near to God in their daily lives. The songs we choose for corporate worship each week can be powerful resources in private worship times and in discipleship.

Trait 5: Facilitates a God-focus in corporate worship

Corporate worship is all about giving God the glory He deserves (Psalm 29:2). Our worship times must be centered in God, and celebrate the good news of redemption through the life, death and resurrection of Jesus.

Trait 6: Assists the leadership in fostering spiritual growth of the congregation

The ultimate goal of a worship leader is to assist the pastor and staff in leading the congregation toward maturity in Christ. The weekly worship service—though the biggest and most time-consuming—is only one aspect of that goal. It is also our duty to create a nurturing environment within the teams we lead and in smaller group settings within the church. Many of our worship team members consider the worship ministry their primary point of personal and spiritual contact within the church. Therefore, it's important to implement "member care" as a vital part of the worship ministry. Member care involves ministering to each other, just as any small group or Sunday school class would.

Although it's impossible for the worship leader alone to meet all of the spiritual needs of each worship/tech team member, it's important to set up a system of volunteers within the team to help with things like hospital

Worship Foundry

visitation, organizing meals (for those who are sick, going through a family crisis, or mourning the death of a loved one), prayer, service projects for those inside and outside the team, etc. Galatians 6:2 says, "Carry each other's burdens, and in this way you will fulfill the law of Christ."

Trait 7: Makes Christ known to the local community

Each community has a unique culture and history. Understanding these important aspects will better help us minister to our neighbors. Rick Warren, founding pastor of Saddleback Church in Lake Forest, California, implemented "targeted evangelism" when he did a study several decades ago for his first church plant in Orange County. He created "Saddleback Sam," describing the likely "Mr. South Orange County." Some have come to criticize this approach, feeling that it excludes others. But a good understanding of the community in which we minister is the first step in reaching its citizens for Christ.

Also, many have neglected taking into account the history of a church or community; their preference may be to start from scratch with new ministries, programs, etc. It's always wise, though, to get to know the personality of a church, to discover the assets and victories in its history. The church most likely has an important niche in the community that set it apart from other churches. Maybe it was a solid choir program, a strong children's music program, a yearly event, etc., that helped distinguish it among the others in the community.

As a new minister, tearing out the old and replacing it with the new—all for the sake of "modernizing" the place—may be throwing out the baby with the bath water! So, get to know the history of the church and community you are serving; honor it, seek to understand it, and build on its strengths.

Trait 8: Makes Christ known throughout the world

Matthew 28:19-20 describes the Great Commission clearly: "Therefore go and make disciples of all nations, baptizing them in the name of the Father and of the Son and of the Holy Spirit, and teaching them to obey everything I have commanded you. And surely I am with you always, to the very end of the age."

As the local church, we have an opportunity to enlist our worship teams to reach beyond our community for Christ. Music is a powerful tool in evangelism, and planning for evangelistic opportunities will help fulfill the Great Commission that Jesus imparted to each of us, maybe through a mission trip to another state or a foreign country. Whichever the case, reaching out beyond our walls, borders and continent to the world will always bless those who receive the Gospel, and will surely bless those who carry the message.

Trait 9: Does all for the glory of God

It's amazing how much effort we put into our worship services each week. It can be so daunting that, ironically, we forget that it's all for the glory of God. An offering, be it great or small, is measured by the heart of the giver. So many churches have insufficient means to produce big Sunday morning extravaganzas, while other churches splurge on incredibly expensive tools and world-class events. It's my desire to always consider that we are doing this for the glory of God—from the earliest conception of an idea to the final product. In the end, what we do for God won't be remembered as much as our attitude of worship in the process.

In Luke 21:1-4, Jesus spoke of the widow and her offering: "And He looked up and saw the rich putting their gifts into the treasury, and He saw also a certain poor widow putting in two mites. So He said, 'Truly I say to you that this poor widow has put in more than all; for all these out of their abundance have put in offerings for God, but she out of her poverty put in all the livelihood that she had. (NKJV)'"

It doesn't matter how large the ministry, how many people attend, or how magnificent the church buildings. In the end, it's all about GOD. Our efforts, while attempting to please people—like the grass and the flowers in Isaiah 40—will fade away.

A Game-Changing Prayer

I was recently reminded of a prayer that was spoken many centuries ago by Sir Francis Drake, who sailed around the world for England in 1577. When we echo this prayer from an open heart to God, it can be a game-changer for our lives. Many choose to experience life from the grandstands: cheering others on as they make their way around the track. My personal goal is to live fully

Worship Foundry

engaged in a faith-filled, on-the-field experience. I don't want to vicariously experience someone else's life, but instead, to trust God for my own unique journey. Following God, as described in this prayer, is not a journey for the faint of heart. He will give us the strength we need for the journey!

As Sir Francis Drake set out on an important voyage, he may have been afraid of challenges and setbacks, but his main concern was to be fully engaged in the God-journey chosen for him by the Creator. We as Christ-followers have a custom God-journey designed for us as well. The question is: Are we willing to let God strip away every hindrance that inhibits us from reaching our goals, to allow God to shake up our lives when complacency sets in? Read this prayer and dare to echo its dangerous plea:

Disturb us, Lord, when
We are too pleased with ourselves,
When our dreams have come true
Because we dreamed too little,
When we arrived safely
Because we sailed too close to the shore.
Disturb us, Lord, when
With the abundance of things we possess
We have lost our thirst
For the waters of life;
Having fallen in love with life,
We have ceased to dream of eternity
And in our efforts to build a new earth,
We have allowed our vision
Of the new Heaven to dim.
Disturb us, Lord, to dare more boldly,
To venture on wilder seas
Where storms will show Your mastery;
Where losing sight of land,
We shall find the stars.
We ask you to push back
The horizons of our hopes;
And to push back the future
In strength, courage, hope, and love.
This we ask in the name of our Captain,
Who is Jesus Christ.

Jamie Harvill

It has been extremely difficult at times for me and my family as we decided early on to walk in faith, and believe that if God leads us to an opportunity, He will supply the means to see us through to the end. It's a scary thing to ask for God to "disturb us," but thrilling to see Him perform miracles along the way. As God invites us to join Him on this magnificent journey, the payoff will be well worth the sacrifice. Paul wrote of this "payoff" in Hebrews 10:35-39:

"So do not throw away your confidence; it will be richly rewarded. You need to persevere so that when you have done the will of God, you will receive what he has promised. For, 'In just a little while, he who is coming will come and will not delay.' And 'But my righteous one will live by faith. And I take no pleasure in the one who shrinks back.' But we do not belong to those who shrink back and are destroyed, but to those who have faith and are saved."

You may be a young student just starting out, or perhaps in the middle of your career. You may be full-time, part-time, or even a volunteer worship leader. In any case, it's exciting to be a part of God's plan for a local church, and it's an honor to serve alongside other leaders who are sowing into people's lives.

The opportunity to serve God in the local church, or on the mission field, can be an extremely fulfilling faith-adventure. God wants to fill us with fuel— purpose, hope, provision and strength—for the journey.

I pray that the rest of this book helps you be the best worship leader possible. Bon voyage!

SECTION 2:
FOUNDATIONS FOR WORSHIP MINISTRY

Worship and Virtue

When we whole-heartedly worship God:

1. We acknowledge Who He is (Creator, Sustainer, Redeemer, Healer, Restorer, worthy of praise)
2. We acknowledge who we are (incomplete apart from His presence, provision, forgiveness, love and guidance)
3. We confess our absolute dependence upon Him

Worship Is All of Life

Worship isn't limited to singing or the song set before the sermon. Rather as an act of continual prayer, worship is meant to fill each moment of every day (1 Thessalonians 5:17). Our bodies were intended to be *temples* of worship (1 Corinthians 6:19-20) and, according to Scripture, every believer is a *priest*, whose duty is to bring sacrifices to God (1 Peter 2:9). We offer ourselves to God in worship—living sacrifices, holy and pleasing to Him (Romans 12:1-2).

The priests of the Old Testament took turns serving in the Temple, facilitating worship 24-hours a day. The role of the priest in the Old Testament was to minister to God on behalf of the people and minister to the people on the behalf of God. Now, even in this modern post-New Testament era of worship, we must, like the Temple priests, serve God and worship Him on a continual basis. So, worship is meant to be an around-the-clock exercise. During our day, as we go about our business, we offer

Jamie Harvill

our joys, our fears, our jobs, our friends, our family, our wills, and our future to Him as we worship.

The Worship of God is Virtue

Virtue is not only equated with moral excellence, goodness and righteousness, but with purpose. In classic philosophical terms (teleology) it means: to fulfill the *purpose* for which something was created. In other words:

- The virtue of a *hammer* is to drive or extract nails
- The virtue of a *guitar* is to create music
- The virtue of *lawn mower* is to cut grass

If we misuse something—an acoustic guitar to drive a stake in the ground, for instance—the guitar will most likely end up in splinters, and the stake will probably not have budged an inch. Living in sin—deliberate disobedience to the known will of God—is a misuse of our *lives*, and it's the direct opposite of virtue. Sin leaves us empty, frustrated and bereft of the good things God intends for us. Walking away from God leaves us broken and splintered like the acoustic guitar. But instead, if we invest our lives in the purposes of God, walking with Him and exalting Him daily, we are changed, and the world around us will be affected.

Since we were created to exalt God and fellowship with Him, worship is the *ultimate virtue* for humanity. Therefore in worship, we are fulfilling our *true purpose*—mentally, spiritually and physically. It's a great honor for a leader to facilitate worship in the congregation, to raise up a kingdom of priests in the church.

Think On These Things

Philippians 4:8 "Finally, brothers and sisters, whatever is true, whatever is noble, whatever is right, whatever is pure, whatever is lovely, whatever is admirable—if anything is excellent or praiseworthy—think about such things."

2 Corinthians 10:5 "We demolish arguments and every pretension that sets itself up against the knowledge of God,

Worship Foundry

and we take captive every thought to make it obedient to Christ."

<u>1 Corinthians 6:12</u> "'I have the right to do anything,' you say—but not everything is beneficial. 'I have the right to do anything'—but I will not be mastered by anything."

<u>Proverbs 3:7</u> "Do not be wise in your own eyes; fear the Lord and shun evil."

<u>John 8:31</u> "To the Jews who had believed him, Jesus said, 'If you hold to my teaching, you are really my disciples.'"

I once visited a newly-planted church in the suburbs of Pittsburgh, Pennsylvania, to teach about worship. Among the attendees was a marriage and family counselor, Bill Halle, who served on the worship team as a volunteer. During one of my teaching sessions Bill interjected a very interesting perspective on worship from his years of study and experience in counseling.

Bill is the founder and CEO of *Grace Youth and Family Foundation* in Butler, Pennsylvania. Over the years he has worked with many broken and battered people. As a therapist he has helped lead many to wholeness through Christ. The thoughts he shared can help those of us who are leaders to better understand the importance of worship in the church. I later asked him to write down those thoughts, and I share them with you here:

"In the realm of behavioral science and counseling, we know that human emotions do not know the difference between what is right and what is wrong, or what is real and what is not real. Our emotions simply respond to the stimuli on which we choose to focus our thoughts. If we fill our minds with Satan's lies/error, our emotions will ultimately lead us to choices of sinful behavior. If we fill our minds with God's word/truth our emotions will ultimately lead us to choices of Godly behavior. This is the importance of the simple principles found in Philippians 4:8, 2 Corinthians 10:5 and 1 Corinthians 6:12. It is on what we focus our conscious thoughts that will make all the difference in our life experience and walk of faith (Proverbs 3:7, John 8:31)."

Halle goes on to say, "Satan intentionally leads people's emotions to sinful behavior with error. We as worship leaders must be equally if

33

Jamie Harvill

not more intentional about leading people's emotions to godly behavior through the truth of His word."

Effective worship leaders help foster emotional and spiritual health in the church. It's not a worship leader's job to simply produce a music set each week, but also to partner with the pastor and the church leadership to raise up fully engaged, 24-hour worshipers!

A Worshiping Church

My earliest childhood recollection of church and worship music came from the times I visited the First Church of the Nazarene with my grandmother in Anaheim, California. Growing up in a non-Christian home, my experience of church was limited to attending Sunday school classes a few times, an occasional visit to vacation Bible school in the summer, and sitting next to Grandma while she sang those old songs from the Nazarene hymnal.

I remember colored light streaming in through the brilliant stained-glass windows on both sides of the sanctuary. The pulpit stood between an organ and a piano—the only instruments used to accompany the choir. Gentle breezes from an open window caught the scent of mothballs from the choir robes, and the cacophony of perfume and aftershave from the squeaky-clean, finely-dressed congregation flowed to my senses and into the deep recesses of my memory. The pastor preached dramatic sermons, but all I could remember were his hand gestures and booming voice, not the message.

Nevertheless, I remember Grandma's passion for God. She cried when she prayed, she knew Bible verses by heart and knew the songs in the hymn book, too. I was impressed with her dedication, faith, love and devotion to the Lord. This was my earliest impression of true worship.

When I received Christ in the spring of 1975, I knew little about church, but I knew that Emma Marie Rye, my grandmother, was a true believer. I also consider my wife, Brenda, to be the greatest example of a devoted Christian that I have ever met. My earliest concepts of worship helped to

Jamie Harvill

develop what I later learned must be the primary focus in a believer's life and of the Church.

The Priority of Worship

The Doxology—the glory of God—must be central in our philosophy of ministry. God's worship is the divine goal of His redemptive work. Salvation is not an end in itself. The praise of God is the highest good.

In Ephesians 1:11-14, the Apostle Paul writes of the centrality of worship :

> *"In him we were also chosen, having been predestined according to the plan of him who works out everything in conformity with the purpose of his will, in order that we, who were the first to hope in Christ, might be for the **praise of his glory**. And you also were included in Christ when you heard the word of truth, the gospel of your salvation. Having believed, you were marked in him with a seal, the promised Holy Spirit, who is a deposit guaranteeing our inheritance until the redemption of those who are God's possession—**to the praise of his glory**. (emphasis mine)"*

Author Ronald B. Allen, in his book *The Wonder of Worship*, writes: "Our salvation—as glorious as that is—is not God's final purpose. Our salvation is designed to bring more glory to God." He goes on to say, "In this context we find the biblical significance of all other ministries. We don't read Scripture just to know more about God's revelation. We don't involve ourselves in evangelism just to lead more people to salvation. We don't promote world missions just to reach the lost. These ministries and many others have wonderful meaning in their own terms; but all of them, when done in the power of God's Spirit and to God's glory, have one end—the worship of God."

Charles H. Spurgeon (1834-1892) proclaimed the *power of worship*. He made this clear in a sermon from *The Metropolitan Tabernacle Pulpit*:

- [Worship] is an open avowal (affirmation, declaration) of our faith in God and our belief in prayer
- [Worship] secures unity in prayer

- [Worship] is a great means of quickening (encouragement)
- [Worship] blesses the world (God's manifest presence in a world of darkness)
- [Worship] is a rehearsal for the service of heaven

Rubel Shelly, from the book *In Search of Wonder: A call to worship renewal*, speaks of the importance of corporate worship: "[It] brings us into the presence of God's people and drives away feelings of isolation and loneliness. Corporate worship draws us into a community of faith—past, present and future."

A Foundation Made of Sand

We've established that the worship of God must be the predominant activity of the Church and in the life of every believer. In some churches, however, the powerful personality and preaching style of a pastor, or the singing or instrumental talent of a worship leader, may distract the congregation from the *true* focus of worship. Any ministry that is built on the merits of a person is destined to crumble like a foundation made of sand.

In the book, *The Gift of Worship*, C. Welton Gaddy writes about an interesting account of a 19th century preacher who took the pulpit as a guest at Plymouth Church in Brooklyn, New York. The church's renowned pastor, Henry Ward Beecher, was away on this particular Sunday. When the guest preacher got up to the platform, many got up to leave. Seeing the rapid flight of those exiting, he raised his hand and said, "All those who came to worship Henry Ward Beecher may now withdraw—all who came to worship God may remain."

Gaddy goes on to say: "The people of God gather around the Word of God—the Word revealed in Scripture and the Word incarnate in Christ—to worship God. If people assemble only around preaching or a preacher, worship will not occur and that fellowship will not endure as a Christian church. As an act of worship, preaching contributes immensely to both the meaning of worship and the growth of the church. But preaching cannot singularly carry the burden of sustaining either worship or a church of worshipers."

In today's North American church culture, where contemporary styles of worship and high caliber music production is sought after, there is a great tendency to put talented musicians and performers on a pedestal, too.

Jamie Harvill

Preaching vs. Music in Worship

The balance in preaching and music has been challenged in many churches over the last few decades. Many would argue that preaching the Word must be the *focal point* in the worship service. But as established so far, the *worship of God* must be the preeminent focus for the worship service, and that doesn't mean that music equals worship, or that music is equal to the Word of God. Preaching and singing are both important components of worship.

The preaching of God's Word is a vital component of a worship service. In Colossians 3:16 Paul writes: "Let the message of Christ dwell among you richly *as* you teach and admonish one another with all wisdom through psalms, hymns, and songs from the Spirit, singing to God with gratitude in your hearts."

TECHNOLOGY, TRADITION AND CHANGE

We are living in an age of rapid change. Communications have advanced at lightning speed. Modern life involves inevitable, constant change. New hi-tech products are becoming increasingly affordable, and children of the past few generations only know a world where cell phones, laptops, tablet computers, entertainment consoles and digital music are commonplace.

Technology Has Benefited Christianity

Dr. Dale B. Sims is a professor of Management Information Systems at Dallas Baptist University. In a paper entitled *The Effect of Technology on Christianity: Blessing or Curse?*, Dr. Sims raises interesting discussion points regarding technology and the Church: "Technology has given Christianity a voice to reach a world-wide audience. Historically there have been advances for Christianity when there have been advances in technology."

Sims points out in his paper some important milestones of technology that have impacted the Church in a positive way:

> **Pax Romana:** "It was described by Edward Gibbon in *The Decline and Fall of the Roman Empire* as a time of "peace for Rome," which existed at the time of Christ and played

Jamie Harvill

a large role in the spread of the Gospel. Technology that created good roads for transportation, that bolstered the strongest army in the world to enforce relatively peaceful times, and stabilized governments for common laws, common language, and common culture allowed a small group of Christians to become a large following in a single generation."

The Printing Press: It has enabled ideas to flow rapidly and in large quantities to very large audiences. William Tyndale translated the Bible into English and had it printed and distributed in the early 1500s.

Scientific Advancements and Philosophy: Blaise Pascal, Isaac Newton, and Samuel Morse were scientists who held Christianity and the Bible in the highest regard.

Digital Technology: "The Gospel has the potential to reach millions in a nano-second, for instance, and digital technology allows e-books and other electronic materials to be distributed without cutting down a single tree. Much like the Roman roads—which enabled the spread of the Gospel to be preached throughout the world for the first missionaries—the digital revolution has enabled the Gospel to find its way into the remotest parts of the globe."

Certainly technology has its critics. Some say that telecommunications have allowed humans to avoid the actual "face-to-face" interaction in missions, that pop culture promotes *style* over *substance*, and that technology has created a worship experience of isolation and entertainment. As Simms went on to ask in his paper: Has technology been allowed to affect the Church in reshaping the Message to fit the mold of culture? Does technology create distractions that draw us away from the message of Christ?

If we are resisting change because of personal prejudice or preference, we need to seek a change of heart. Author Ronald Allen says, "There is nothing spiritual about engaging in change, if it's just change. But when change is motivated by a love for God and a desire for His worship to

Worship Foundry

be more effective among the changing needs of people, then it may be wonderfully led and blessed by the Holy Spirit."

The Amish: a radical response to changing culture

The Amish are a Christian religious sect. They can be found in many parts of the U.S., and are known for taking their style cues from sometime back in the 18th and 19th centuries: the men, with long beards, simple black and white clothing and large hats; the women, with plain long dresses and head coverings.

For the most part, the Amish are known to refrain from using electricity and, even in the 21st century, still travel by horse and buggy. Their founding leader, Jacob Amman, led the charge to split from the Mennonites in 1693, and after immigrating to Pennsylvania in the 18th century, the Amish took on their current cultural distinction.

Their aversion to progress and technology, for the sake of purity, has not only affected their dress but their whole way of life. In their culture the individual is second to the group, church, or family. Because of this, they avoid anything that would steer the faithful away from their belief system. Some have left the fold, only to be "shunned" or excommunicated. The Amish culture is a radical response to changing culture. As we have seen, many respond to technology and change as an affront to their traditional system of beliefs.

Technology: Orthopraxy vs. Orthodoxy

There is a theological distinction between correct belief, *orthodoxy*, and correct action, *orthopraxy*. It can be said "correct belief" compels "correct action/activity." Regarding the "practice" of the Christian faith, the Apostle Paul, in Ephesians 4:1, states: "I therefore, a prisoner for the Lord, urge you to walk in a manner worthy of the calling to which you have been called. (ESV)" Romans 8:29 says: "For those whom he foreknew he also predestined to be conformed to the image of his Son, in order that he might be the firstborn among many brothers. (ESV)" The sticky situation in which many find themselves is: By which prescribed method are we able to be "conformed to the image of his Son?" Can certain methods or technologies be morally corrupt? If we have our "orthodoxy" correct, can we be compromised by our "orthopraxy?" I will leave that up to you to decide!

41

Jamie Harvill

Worship Wars

The worship revolution and the Jesus Movement, beginning on the West Coast of the United States in the mid to latter part of the '60s, made its way across North America. Many were converted to Christ during this time and, as a result, the youth culture began to apply its rock music style to their songs of praise to God. Guitars and drums began to take the place of pianos and organs in churches like Calvary Chapel of Costa Mesa, California. All these years later there continues to be resistance toward rock music in some churches and denominations, many stating that rock music is not "sacred." Still, the "war" rages on.

West Coast pastor Rick Warren says in response to this divisive issue, "The style of music you use in your services will be one of the most critical (and controversial) you make in the life of your church. It may also be the most influential factor in determining who your church reaches for Christ and whether or not your church grows. To insist that all 'good' music was written in Europe two hundred years ago is cultural elitism. There certainly isn't any biblical basis for that view...Churches also need to admit that no particular style of music is 'sacred.' What makes a song sacred is its message."

Change is inevitable for any society, community or church, and it must be carried out with patience, diligent preparation, and through much prayer.

So I'm A Worship Leader—Now What?

A friend called the other day to tell me he was just offered the job of worship leader in his church. Apparently the person who held that position for several years had abruptly decided to move on. My friend is a wonderful musician and singer, a Godly man, and a great husband and father. With past worship leading experience, he seems to be a great candidate. But with this opportunity, he now faces the challenge of holding down a regular 40-hour-per-week job while handling the demanding leadership duty at church. He is hopeful but I sense his anxiety.

Some churches have been forced to pare down their operations to accommodate income challenges. Volunteers are being called upon more and more to fill positions once occupied by paid staff. If you've been asked by your pastor to take a worship-leadership role in your church, you must be honest with yourself about what the job truly demands. It's a great responsibility that requires character, leadership and skill. Here are a few things to consider before committing to the job:

1. **It is a <u>people</u> related job.** If you are not excited about leading, equipping, serving or generally being around people, this job isn't for you. It is a team sport!

2. **It is a <u>spiritual</u> role.** Your positive Christian testimony and your walk with Christ are very important to the job. People are watching

you, *on* and *off* stage. Do you behave one way at work or home, and another way at church? As a spiritual leader, you are an extension of the pastor's pulpit and care ministries. Many of the people in your church will see you at the pulpit almost as much as they see the pastor. Are you ready for such a task?

3. **It requires <u>musical and technical abilities</u>.** Being an effective worship leader requires basic knowledge and skill in instrumental and vocal music, plus some performing skills. It helps if you know some technical basics like how sound, lighting and video systems work. You are essentially the "producer" of the service; you pull it all together. You don't need to be an expert, but you need to know how everything works together in the service. If you don't have experience in some of the areas mentioned, you need to be willing to learn.

4. **It is a <u>leadership</u> role.** You prepare, come early, stay late, solve problems, set vision and direction for your team, encourage, correct, make difficult decisions, and usually take the blame when things go wrong—even when it's not your fault. You must understand what the pastor expects from you as a leader. If you're a volunteer, most of your preparation will be done at home, after work, and you will have to be a self-manager.

5. **It is a <u>servant</u> role.** The job of worship leader isn't to showcase your wonderful singing ability, your incredible songwriting or smoking guitar licks. You are there to serve, and the ultimate aim is to help enrich the relationship between your congregation and God. You must serve with skill, excellence, love, patience, humility and grace—even when you are tired and don't feel like it.

Before taking any church position, make sure you know what's expected of you. Realize, too, that even if you are given a job description with an employee manual, there are still many unseen political processes, cultural behavior requirements and social mores—particular to each organization—that you have yet to discover (These unwritten rules don't come in the form of a book or list, but are usually acquired through paying close attention to the unspoken expectations of your job—this takes a heavy dose of *emotional intelligence*. Daniel Goleman elaborates on this in his book of the same name).

Pastor/ Worship Leader Relationship

It's important to communicate with the pastor as often as possible. I don't expect to be best friends, but it's a benefit to you and the congregation to enjoy working together. It's important to establish some kind of weekly meeting to discuss vision, future sermon topics, or simply to connect on a personal, spiritual level—maybe even to discuss technical needs, staging, video ideas, sermon theme support, special events, set lists, stage transitions, etc. It's also a good time to evaluate last week's service and to make changes and improvements for the future.

I have a saying that holds true in most church situations: "You can't go faster than the pastor!" That means we as worship leaders take a subordinate role to the pastor. We are there to serve, encourage and support. They set the pace—we follow.

Worship Resources

As worship leaders, we are not alone. There are many websites and blogs that bring encouragement and instruction. The following are a handful of services that will get you started:

<u>CCLI</u>

A worship leader spends a large amount of their time pouring over songs, CDs, music books, etc., to choose music for the team. Many leaders are not aware that it's illegal to make photo copies of songs without the permission of the publisher. Song writers and publishers make their living through royalties generated from performances of their work. Churches must obtain licenses for printing lyrics in the bulletin, projecting them onto a screen, making copies of songs for rehearsal, and music to be used in videos, among other things. There is a service available to worship leaders to obtain these rights. Your church should consider establishing a relationship with Christian Copyright Licensing International, *CCLI*, for several reasons:

Jamie Harvill

1. To procure a church copyright license. This covers over 200,000 worship songs for congregational singing. There are licenses for special events and mobile licenses for traveling ministries. The reality is, churches must pay for the rights to project words on a screen and provide lyrics in printed form.

2. As a great resource for chord charts, lead sheets: *SongSelect*®. This subscription service features lyrics, samples and transposable lead sheets, chord sheets and hymn/vocal sheets for churches to customize and print.

3. To find a list of the top 25 worship songs in the U.S. (and all over the world). This is a great place to find new songs, too. Of course your church's music style will dictate which of those songs you can use. But the top songs—the ones used the most in churches—are listed and updated here.

Christian Copyright Solutions

As the website states: "Christian Copyright Solutions (CCS) was launched in 2001 out of a desire to provide online solutions to simplify the copyright clearance process. 'Since that time we have helped more than 2,000 churches become copyright compliant, ranging from small local churches to some of the largest churches in the country, including Saddleback Church, Northpoint Church, Gateway Church and Willow Creek Church.'" CCS's Founder and CVO, Susan Fontaine Godwin, is an educator and long-time member of the Christian arts community with many years of experience in the Christian media industry, church copyright administration and copyright management. Some of CCS's services include:

WORSHIPcast: There is a religious service exemption in U.S. copyright law that allows churches to perform copyrighted music during religious services. The exemption does not cover the re-transmission of those services over radio, television or the internet. If your church's services include copyrighted music, you need a church streaming license to webcast those services.

PERFORMmusic: A license which covers a wide range of performances of live and pre-recorded music outside of religious services.

PERMISSIONSplus: A comprehensive copyright clearance process

Worship Foundry

for church recording projects, DVDs, rehearsal CDs, showing movies to a public audience, etc.

You will find more useful worship resources, updated on a regular basis, at www.worshipfoundry.com.

SECTION 3:
TEAM BUILDING

BUILDING A TEAM AROUND AN ORGANIZATIONAL PLAN

Aubrey Malphurs leads a group that helps churches, non-profit organizations, marketplace companies and leaders around the globe. He describes team building as: "The careful, patient construction of a team of people around the organizational vision for the purpose of implementing the vision." With this we see some very important things to consider when choosing our own team:

1. Be **careful** and **patient** when choosing the team:
    - *Careful*: make sure the people you choose have the qualities you need to fulfill the mission of the ministry team. Ask questions like: What is their history? Are they Christ-followers? Do they attend your church regularly? How is their reputation in the community? Are they adequate as musicians, singers or technicians to help fulfill your goals and standard of excellence?
    - *Patient*: don't be in a rush to bring someone on to the team. Set up a fair system that adequately helps to display their musical, technical, spiritual and personal qualities in an interview/audition process, and choose members who will, to the best of their ability, uphold the values and standards you establish in your ministry.

Jamie Harvill

2. Build the team around an **organizational vision**:
   - Establish a plan for where you want to go with the team
   - Map out how you will get there
   - Communicate a very clear description of what is expected from each member
   - Establish a system of values from which to measure growth, success, and effectiveness
   - Take action on ways to improve organizational processes, the team's effectiveness, and the goal of Godly character and excellence in all things

To properly construct a ministry plan, it's helpful to describe what is to be accomplished through the ministry. In other words, how is the "end product" of our ministry to look?

George Barna, in his book *The Habits of Highly Effective Churches,* describes a vibrant, healthy church as: "[a place] where the people are implementing Christianity more and more deeply, both on the corporate and individual levels. They are people who worship God on a regular basis. They are people who constantly introduce non-Christians to Christ on a regular basis. They are learning and applying principles and truths of the Christian faith to their lives. They are developing significant relationships with other believers, befriending, encouraging and holding each other accountable. They joyfully contribute their material possessions to ministries and individuals in need, for the glory of God. And they devote their time and energy to helping disadvantaged people. Cumulatively, these behaviors represent the Church in its fullest manifestation."

Thom S. Rainer, president and CEO of *LifeWay Christian Resources,* describes five areas of priority in an effective church:

Evangelism   Discipleship   Fellowship   Ministry   Worship

The worship ministry must contribute to the success of all five priorities of the church. Therefore, we must ask important questions when developing an organizational plan:

- Has our current worship ministry been effective in contributing to a healthy, vibrant church?
- How will our worship ministry assist the other four priorities?

Worship Foundry

- What are current unmet needs as to the worship ministry in our church?
- Do the pastor and leadership agree on the perceived needs in the church?
- If change is necessary, how will it affect the congregation?
- Is our vision big enough? If it is within our grasp to accomplish the vision, then it's probably too small and limits God!

Determining Mission and Vision

To help develop an organizational plan for our ministry, Thom Rainer separates two distinct areas: **mission** and **vision**. He states that *"mission is the primary purpose in which all Christian churches should be involved; these purposes typically include evangelism, discipleship, fellowship, ministry and worship."* Therefore, he asserts *mission* should *never* change in the life of a church. On the other hand, he continues, *vision* is "God's *specific* plan for a specific church at a specific time," and because of this, *vision* is *always* changing.

In short, we must create an *unchanging* list of values in the *mission statement*, pertaining to the area of worship ministry, as well as develop a *vision statement* concerning the *ever-changing* challenges and needs in our church.

In the process, it's helpful to create a short, distinct statement that can be easily *taught* and effectively *caught* by the congregation and especially the worship team. The development of a *mission statement* and a *vision statement* for the worship ministry is vital to staying "on track" with ministry goals and values, and helps keep financial resources and volunteers focused on core initiatives. Even if the senior pastor or other leadership do not require you to develop a ministry plan, it's to your advantage to do so. Our influence as a leader will cross over into other areas of the church in which we serve...it may even flow upward to affect the head honcho!

When You Inherit a Worship Ministry

Several years ago I helped start a church. This particular fellowship broke away from a well-established church that had been around for several generations. When the church divided, most of the worship team left to help form the new one. The pastor who was leaving to start this new work

Jamie Harvill

invited me to be their worship leader. Therefore, I had the difficult task of starting a new team with old members—it was much like the proverbial "old-dog-new-trick" scenario. We began to formulate a direction and to start building an infrastructure as a new church.

After a few months, the lack of leadership with the previous music director began to show. As most of the members were "grandfathered" into the new system, they had a tough time accepting the new requirements I was imposing, such as not being late to rehearsal, and that no one could miss rehearsal and show up to play on Sunday morning. It was up to me as their new leader to set things right, to make some hard decisions and establish even more focused requirements for the ministry than what they were accustomed.

Early on we began broadcasting the services on a local TV station. It wasn't long before I received comments from viewers in the community who saw the service on TV, but didn't attend the church. They mentioned having seen a particular member on our worship team who had a negative reputation in the community. The person in question was living a dual life: one way at church and another way in the community. After looking into the matter, and confirming that the information was true, I felt we couldn't continue with this person on the team. (I believe that as leaders and worship team members we must conduct ourselves in a responsible manner, honoring Christ at all times, whether it's on or off stage). I will pick back up on this story in a few moments.

• • •

I don't believe that the pulpit area of a church is any more "holy" than another area. But when someone takes center-stage on the church platform, it's best that they are fully supported by the leadership, and that which flows from the pulpit microphone is honorable, representative of the Word of God and the philosophy of the church. More importantly, when one is on the worship team their behavior is expected to be commensurate with the Christ-centered life. (This is why I am opposed to inviting random people up to the stage during a service to speak or give testimony. It's always good to coach an inexperienced speaker before they stand behind the pulpit to read Scripture, give a testimony, or bring a message. The lack of experience in speaking, annoying gestures and unedited content, can take a congregation "hostage," and has the potential to destroy the trust of the audience and the momentum of a service).

Worship Foundry

The Christ-centered Life

Different denominations have a wide variety of criteria for what they define *good Christian behavior*. Therefore, to make a determination that is not garbled up with religious *dos, don'ts* and *preferences*, I turn to Scripture for my definition. In Galatians 5:22-23, Paul describes a Spirit-filled person as one who's life produces the "fruit" of the Spirit: "But the fruit of the Spirit is love, joy, peace, forbearance, kindness, goodness, faithfulness, gentleness and self-control. Against such things there is no law." When one professes Christ as Savior, and makes the public declaration through believer's baptism, the way to truly see the evidence of the indwelling Christ is through the fruit their lives produce.

The best we can do as leaders is to trust the candidate's profession of faith, and that we see the evidence of a transformed life. We can be confident when the candidate is actively:

- Growing in relationship with Jesus Christ
- Connecting in Biblical community
- Serving in God-given ministry
- Sharing the message of Jesus Christ

• • •

Back to the situation I mentioned previously when I had to ask a team member to step down...After discussing the problem of our wayward worship team member with my senior pastor, we thought it best to ask the entire worship team to step down so we could start again from scratch. Many felt slighted and left the new fellowship, while others stayed to follow through with the requisite interview and audition process we subsequently implemented. This meant I had to lead worship all by myself with an acoustic guitar for a few months. We finally were able to introduce a band and singers back to our worship services after establishing a new and comprehensive set of requirements for the team. We also established an annual seminar that each member was required to attend, with regular audition opportunities throughout the year, and a commitment form to sign.

I learned a big lesson through this journey: that it is *imperative* for leaders to construct a worship team with the *proper* people involved, built

Jamie Harvill

on a firm foundation of Biblical principles and operational guidelines. You may have inherited a worship team like I did. Whatever situation you are currently in, it's up to you as the leader to build a solid, communicable set of guidelines for the worship ministry and the team, as soon as possible.

THE TEAM SELECTION PROCESS

Musical ability is obviously a trait to look for in a prospective team member, but there are several other considerations. Possible candidates must understand that they be at least as proficient as those who are already on the team. Since talent is never enough, here are the four areas from which to consider a worship team candidate: **Spirituality, Personality, Musicality** and **Technicality**.

We must recruit the most effective people for the worship team. Let's start with the most important consideration.

Spirituality

The candidate must:

Be a Christ-follower

> 2 Corinthians 6:14-18
> "Do not be yoked together with unbelievers. For what do righteousness and wickedness have in common? Or what fellowship can light have with darkness? What harmony is there between Christ and Belial? Or what does a believer have in common with an unbeliever? What agreement is

Jamie Harvill

there between the temple of God and idols? For we are the temple of the living God."

Have a heart for ministry to the Lord and His kingdom

1 Chronicles 15:1-2
"After David had constructed buildings for himself in the City of David, he prepared a place for the ark of God and pitched a tent for it. Then David said, "No one but the Levites may carry the ark of God, because the LORD chose them to carry the ark of the LORD and to minister before him forever."

Nehemiah 12:27-29:
"At the dedication of the wall of Jerusalem, the Levites were sought out from where they lived and were brought to Jerusalem to celebrate joyfully the dedication with songs of thanksgiving and with the music of cymbals, harps and lyres. The musicians also were brought together from the region around Jerusalem—from the villages of the Netophathites, from Beth Gilgal, and from the area of Geba and Azmaveth, for the musicians had built villages for themselves around Jerusalem."

(Other Scripture passages to consider: Romans 12:3-8; 1 Peter 4:7-11)

Be continually growing in Christ

Ephesians 4:14-15
"Then we will no longer be infants, tossed back and forth by the waves, and blown here and there by every wind of teaching and by the cunning and craftiness of people in their deceitful scheming. Instead, speaking the truth in love, we will grow to become in every respect the mature body of him who is the head, that is, Christ."

Worship Foundry

Not be a recent convert

1 Timothy 3:6
"He must not be a recent convert, or he may become conceited and fall under the same judgment as the devil."

Have a good reputation

1 Timothy 3:7
"He must also have a good reputation with outsiders, so that he will not fall into disgrace and into the devil's trap."

Personality

We must also consider **Personal Qualities**. The candidate must:

- Be a team player
- Understand and honor authority
- Be responsible
- Be punctual
- Be courteous to others
- Be prepared musically and technically for rehearsal and performance
- Show grace to others in rehearsal
- Have a servant's attitude- "others first"

Musicality

In choosing team members, we must also consider **Musical Qualities**. The candidate must:

- Exhibit continued growth in musicianship
- Be at least as good as those who are already on the team
- Exhibit natural instrumental and/or vocal ability
- Appreciate a wide variety of musical styles and expressions, but have the ability to excel in the primary musical style expressed by the church
- Pursue excellence

Jamie Harvill

> Psalm 33:1-3: "Sing joyfully to the LORD, you righteous; it is fitting for the upright to praise him. Praise the LORD with the harp; make music to him on the ten-stringed lyre. Sing to him a new song; play skillfully, and shout for joy."

Technicality

In choosing team members for the tech team, we must consider **Technical Qualities**. The candidate must:

- **Be adept at problem solving**
- **Have an aptitude for operating computers, software and various kinds of equipment related to church music production, staging and/or video production; ability to do basic equipment maintenance is a plus**
- **Have a servant's heart**
- **Be willing to learn new technologies**
- **Pursue excellence**

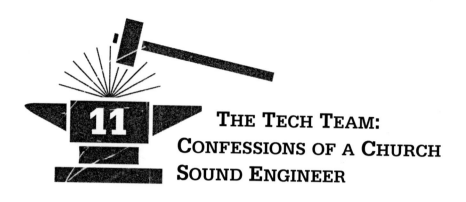

THE TECH TEAM: CONFESSIONS OF A CHURCH SOUND ENGINEER

Andy Bussey, a sound engineer, technology design consultant and personal friend, has been working in church technology and with tech teams for many years. I met Andy while we both were teaching at conferences around the world with various worship companies. Andy has been on staff at major churches across the U.S., and knows the daily frustrations, triumphs and challenges of a growing church.

As a musician, I find that there can be a barrier between the worlds of music and the tech. Sometimes we can barely get on the same page in order to communicate effectively. But when we connect, the results can be astounding!

Andy Bussey is a talented engineer, but has a deep understanding of working with people and building teams.

Andy likes to joke about the differences between musicians and technical people: coming from two different worlds, sometimes we can drive each other crazy in the process of creating music. But by necessity, we must cooperate.

In a recent conversation, Andy explained, "What we do as technicians is to bring together the art and the science and try to empower and support the musicians. Musicians tend to dwell in the 'right-brain,' artist area of what they enjoy doing. Technicians tend to lean into that 'left-brain,' logic area. And so crossing that divide, and being able to communicate and understand one another, is sometimes a careful dance!"

Jamie Harvill

Here is a portion of the conversation I had with Andy about the marriage of worship, music, people and technology.

Jamie: "How can technicians and musicians better communicate?"

Andy: "You have to find a language that the two understand. With all the people I've worked with in the past, I've had to [find a common language].The most successful relationships I've had with artists are the ones I've been able to create a common vocabulary and an understanding with. The more you communicate, the more you understand and can help each other."

Jamie: "What's the most important job of a church tech person?"

Andy: "The first and foremost is heart. I've always told people that I prefer somebody who maybe doesn't have a strong technical background, but has a heart for what they want to do, rather than somebody who has all the skill-sets but is lacking the heart or understanding of a servant. In the context of what we do in church, first and foremost, I look for people with heart and a desire for excellence, the desire to serve one another and to come together to accomplish great things the Lord has given us. And then, with that, we can begin to teach, train and equip on the technical side of things."

Jamie: "You've got to have people on the tech and music teams who cooperate with each other."

Andy: "You've got to enjoy [working together] because it's not always easy. You may have a service where the musicians can't hear and the technician is having a hard time, and you get into the trenches of trying to pull stuff off...You need to live together in the trenches, and to be

Worship Foundry

able to enjoy it with one another, and to enjoy the ministry and the fruits of your efforts, and build a team."

Jamie: "At what point in its life does a church need to think about using technology in a serious manner...employing in-ear monitoring, making use of stage lighting and video, for instance?"

Andy: "It's never too late! I often tell small churches they have obstacles that large churches don't have: the proximity of microphones to the main speakers because you're in a small room...the acoustics, and all of the other things they have going against them. I really feel for the small churches. They have a lower budget; they don't have as many resources available to them to buy all of the expensive gear; they have a smaller group of people.

Jamie: "How should small churches go about purchasing gear while looking at future growth?"

Andy: "They need to look at the music they're going to do—the formation of your band: Is it more of a small praise band or is it more of a [traditional] set-up with an acoustic piano and a choir? Looking at all of the ways you're going to use your facilities, and starting to look ahead as far as you can is always best. Look into the technology and have a plan, even though you can't buy everything right now; at least you'll see where you need to be...and all your resources—all your dollars—are in a common direction, toward a common goal, instead of just being scattered, buying things as you really need them."

Jamie: "Is it good to bring in a tech consultant, as opposed to using a local music store, to help your church with its tech needs?"

Andy: "Absolutely! You can't hurt from gaining knowledge. However, you ask a hundred audio engineers how to mic a

Jamie Harvill

piano and you'll get a hundred different answers. You will get a different preference of how to do things with different people. However, the technology—the board, the speakers, and different things—you really can't hurt from experience outside of the music stores. Music store people know their gear and how to sell it—a lot of them just don't understand the application [worship]…The church's application is very unique, You need to get expertise from people who know that kind of genre of using the equipment."

Jamie: "Would it benefit a small church to think about using a digital console?"

Andy: Originally digital consoles were designed for use in a [recording] studio…The needs of a studio are different from those of live sound. They [eventually] designed digital consoles that allowed the end-user to get to things in a live situation. For instance, with EQ, if you have feedback, you need to get to that feedback as fast as possible. But in digital consoles previous to this, [the EQ function] was buried in layers of menus. So finding the right digital console is important, and it allows you to store Friday night's service, Sunday morning's service, or the youth group's, and to re-call all your settings. Gone are the days of having to take pictures [of the settings]. So, really leveraging a well-designed digital console for a live PA in church is a strong mechanism for empowering your volunteers [to help with] all the needs…in your situation."

Jamie: "Let's talk about the trend nowadays of creating video venues and/or satellite campuses."

Andy: "There's a trend back to smaller groups where people can relate to one another. We want to meet the needs of different types of people in different types of venues. So instead of using resources to build one huge building, it was a great strategy for us to build small venues in different communities [Note: Andy is speaking of a church he once

Worship Foundry

served in greater-Pittsburgh, PA]. Some of those small venues are on the same campus—at our large campus we ended up with three venues. Then, we started to create little campuses around the city of Pittsburgh."

Jamie: "Through this multi-venue concept, a church of 10,000—divided up between several campuses, venues and services—can still enjoy the benefits of a large church, while remaining a smaller congregation within their own community. I'm currently serving in a satellite campus, and it seems most churches [like the one I serve] utilize a live worship team. The preaching is then provided from the "main campus" by video. I find that people are already accustomed to looking at video screens during live preaching, anyway. So it isn't a leap for people to adjust to the preaching from a video in another venue."

Jamie: "Moving on to another subject, how do you recruit and train your tech team members?"

Andy: "We had [at the Pittsburgh church] a handful of volunteers who did all the work...our guys got burned out. So we changed the way we thought about our team. Traditionally you'd say, 'We'll look for technical people to recruit.' And we changed the way we thought about that. It's important with leadership in church, and leadership in general...to duplicate ourselves. Often, we get volunteers but we're afraid to let go of some stuff because we're not sure if the volunteer is qualified enough to do it as good [as us]. We had to look at loving people first. There [are] always things that need to get done that can be done by non-technical folks. So, instead of me being the "sound guy" for the church, my job in leadership is to be the guy that lifts up sound guys for the church...my ultimate goal is to get my hands off the board and raise up other people [for the job]...my role has to change in leadership from doing the sound to support others doing the sound— loving on others, and building a team that cares for each

Jamie Harvill

other…People want to start being a part of that team…I raise them from a personal level, then I sow into them for the technical, teaching them how to run sound, [and] how to run lighting. I think it's most important, again, to cultivate the heart, care about people, and then impart the knowledge."

Jamie: "How early should we start technical planning for an upcoming service?"

Andy: "Last week (laughs)! It's very important as a technical person to stay in communication with the musicians and knowing what their needs are. Right after service I ask them how things were, and I start putting a list together of what to work on [in the coming] week. Being able to get in before the next rehearsal, fixing the things that need to be fixed, getting ready for the things that are on the list for rehearsal, and having your ducks in a row, allows you to be right on it. So when the musicians begin to practice and rehearse, you can address any new things that start to come up, rather than scurrying around, fixing things that should have been fixed the week before. Being prepared way in advance is so important, so that you don't have to feel rushed. At crunch time, if you're just starting to address issues you had last Sunday, you're behind the 8-ball—you're way behind. You're not going to have the ability to enjoy and support the worship on Sunday morning."

Jamie: "One last thing: what "golden nugget" can you share that has helped you as a technical person in ministry and worship?"

Andy: "If your [sense of] accomplishment, or the personal value in what you do comes from people telling you you did a good job—that rarely happens for the technical people because the only time they really get noticed is when something goes wrong—it's very difficult when the

Worship Foundry

value of your efforts come from your actions. [I] really need to be able to have a prayer life, and a relationship with the Lord in such a way that I can rejoice in the successes I've had...When I used to do things for the respect of others, I would get very frustrated. Now, my joy comes from serving the Lord. It allows me to trivialize the tough spots, and get a whole lot more joy out of worshiping God with my gifts."

The Audition Process

When the net is cast for new worship team members, hopefully it will return with a variety of candidates from which to choose. Maybe your invitation will glean only a single candidate, maybe none. Still, it's important to have a consistent interview and audition process in place to help choose effective team members.

The system you put into place may be objective, depending on the requirements you choose. But there is also a bit of subjectivity to the process as well. Sometimes people don't do well in an audition and, based on other information at hand, you may feel it's appropriate to give that person a chance or invite them to the team on a trial basis. In any event, there are three phases to implement for bringing new members on the team: The *questionnaire* phase, the *interview* phase, and the *audition* phase.

Phase 1: The Questionnaire

I am convinced that a worship leader can learn a lot about a person from a simple questionnaire. Construct the questionnaire and develop a packet of information for the prospective team member, including a description of what is expected of team members (personal, spiritual, musical, technical, time, etc.), and an organizational structure with ministry mission and vision statements, etc.

Jamie Harvill

You may want to put an ad like this in your church bulletin:

- "Musician needed: Electric guitarist who plays rock, country and pop styles of music, who can also play lead-guitar solos; must have experience reading music charts."
- "Singers needed: Those who not only sing melody, but are also good at singing harmony."

Make the packet available at an information table, or as an online download from your church website, several weeks in advance of the audition. Ask the candidates to read through the materials, and fill out and return the questionnaire as soon as possible (Please see the sample questionnaire at the end of this section).

Depending on the size of the church—and the availability of candidates at any given time—the worship leader must establish a baseline of musical ability (usually *equal to* or *exceeding* current members. It may be necessary to extend an invitation to a lesser-experienced tech person, musician or singer in order to train and ease them into a permanent place on the team). The questionnaire will probably glean enough information to help you decide whether or not to move ahead with an audition.

Phase 2: The Interview

It's courteous to make a phone call to each candidate who fills out a questionnaire, even if you have decided in phase one that they probably won't be suitable as a team member at this point. Encourage them to improve their musical skills, become more active as an attendee in the church, or maybe invite them to reapply at a later time after they've fulfilled your suggestions for improvement.

It's embarrassing and awkward for a candidate (and the leader) to suffer through an audition where the candidate clearly cannot sing in tune or sufficiently play their instrument. The interview process in phase one will help stream-line the audition process—if enough questions are asked—and will help eliminate awkward situations.

Some leaders may balk at specific requests for candidates, saying it would be a *luxury* to have professional-grade players and singers available in their small churches. But the fact is, you'll never get those types of people

Worship Foundry

if you don't specify your needs and pursue that caliber of candidate. Also, talent attracts talent. Highly-skilled people want to be on a team with other skilled players, singers and technicians. The higher your standards, the higher the caliber of candidates will want to be a part of your team.

Do yourself a favor and *aim high*. Eventually, with good leadership, discipline and patience, the stage can be filled with your dream team!

Phase 3: The Audition

After gathering questionnaires and conducting interviews, formal auditions give you the opportunity to see the candidates in action.

The formal audition is best conducted by at least two persons weighing in on the verdict of whether or not to invite a person to the team.

The skill level of a person must be matched by the spiritual and personal qualities listed earlier. Some ministries require a candidate to be a regular attendee of the church for six months before taking the step toward auditioning for the team. Each church must establish its own requirements.

Preparing For the Audition

In advanced of the audition, supply the candidates with charts, mp3s, lyrics and any notes pertaining to songs that you will be using in the audition. This gives them the opportunity to be at their best.

I usually select three songs to use in the audition. From time to time, depending on the ability of the player, I may throw in a "surprise" song to see how they react on the spot to a new piece of material.

It's best when the atmosphere of the audition is casual and encouraging. Here are some things to consider when conducting an audition:

For Band Candidates:

- Supply charts that are typically used in your worship services on a weekly basis

- Choose a variety of songs that demonstrate versatility of style, with various tempos and feels

71

Jamie Harvill

- Make sure the supplied mp3 song samples match the chart. If not, clearly note the changes in advance

- Have the guitarist bring their own instrument and other necessary gear like pedals and an amp (if the church doesn't already supply one). It's best to supply a professional-quality keyboard, and allow the player sufficient time to adjust to it, and to select appropriate sounds for each song

- Let the drummers make necessary adjustments to the house drum kit. Discourage the candidate from using additional cymbals and personal snares during the audition, as this will slow down the process (changing out a kick drum pedal is acceptable, though). Let the drummers know what is included in the church kit

- Audition the candidates with a typical band set-up (drums, bass, electric guitar, acoustic guitar, keyboard, etc.) to adequately judge their ability to play within a rhythm section

- If your team uses a click track or an electronic metronome during performance, let the players know in advance so they can prepare. Help the drummer become familiar with the metronome's settings, or get one of the other players in the band to change tempos on the metronome between songs

- If you are using an in-ear monitor system in your church instead of monitor wedges, let the candidates know to bring their own headphones

- It's acceptable to audition singers with the band, although it is best done separately

- Use a scoring system on a card supplied to each judge, (see a sample score car at the end of this section), rate the candidate's performance on categories such as instrumental ability, chart reading skills, ability to play with the band, etc.

Worship Foundry

- The collective score from the judges, along with the interview and questionnaire materials, will help determine whether or not a candidate is suitable to join the team

For Vocal Candidates:

If a singer hasn't properly documented their singing range—whether they are a bass, tenor, alto or soprano—use the following keyboard diagram to confirm it.

An average singer can find the melody of a song. But the ability to find and stay on a harmony part, without jumping up or down into someone else's range, is a highly sought-after skill.

An able vocal team is one where each member uses their ability to hear and locate individual parts within pitch, and according to their singing range. They have the ability to follow chord changes in a song, to stay relatively transparent within the group sound, and to use little vibrato or noticeable tone coloration. The goal is a pure group tone, without any individual vocal part standing out from the rest.

Since the melody is usually carried by the worship leader, it's best in the audition process to search for good, harmony singers. The mistake some make in the audition process is to pay too much attention to a vocalist's solo voice. To see if a singer is a good group vocalist, audition them in a group.

Here are some helpful suggestions for the vocal audition:

- For **part-one** of the vocal auditions, gather around a piano to determine individual singing ranges

- Listen for the vocalist's speaking range (low or high) to get an approximate range

- Using the chart above, play the piano note at the highest end of the range you determine, ask them to start singing when they feel they can comfortably hit the note as you descend the chromatic scale. Find the lowest note. Write down the results

Jamie Harvill

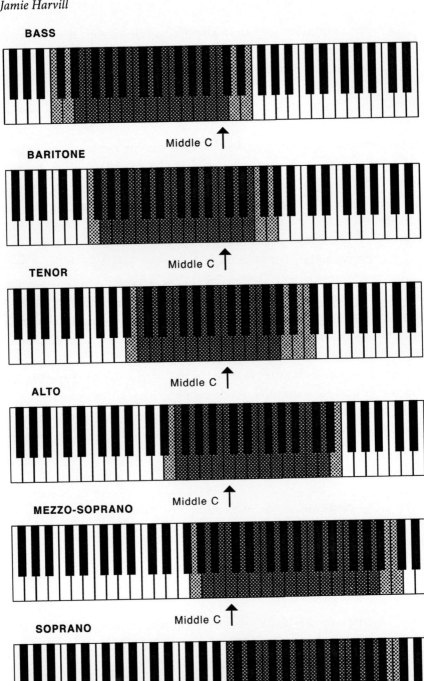

Worship Foundry

- With at least two judges, supply a score card for each candidate and make note of singing ranges and abilities, such as their ability to sing in a group, stage presence, ability to sing solos, etc. (see a sample score card at the end of this section)

- For **part-two** of the vocal audition, create vocal teams (using the judges for parts if necessary) in order to judge their group-singing abilities

- Like the instrumentalists, the collective score from the judges, along with the interview and questionnaire materials, will help determine whether or not a candidate is suitable to join the team

The scoring system will help create a more objective process when choosing new team members. It's tough to reject a candidate with a big heart for the Lord, but whose musical ability just won't make the cut. Again, using more than one judge in the audition process will help to shoulder the responsibility. But it's still up to the leader to make the final decision, to pick up the phone and deliver either good or bad news to the candidate. It's important that each candidate receive a phone call after the audition—they deserve that courtesy. It can be a devastating time for those who don't make the team, so sensitivity and respect is necessary.

THE WORSHIP TEAM AGREEMENT

Team membership requirements, rules and expectations must be established before a candidate joins the team—even before the call goes out for auditions. Each church is unique, so membership requirements may differ from ministry to ministry.

The purpose for a worship team agreement is to establish an understanding between the ministry leadership and the team member. A clear understanding between parties will help eliminate potential problems before they have a chance to materialize (see a sample agreement at the end of this section).

It's good to ask each member to serve for a period of one full year (churches may even have their commitment periods divided into seasons—like school semesters). At the end of that commitment period, the team member can be given the option to recommit.

Make it a priority to go through the *Worship Team Agreement* annually with your team. This can be done effectively during a banquet or a special training session. Go over each item, as well as any revisions that were necessary to make within the year. Give a deadline for each team member to pray about a new commitment cycle, then have them sign and return the form.

Jamie Harvill

The Currency for Volunteers: Appreciation

Most of our teams are made up of volunteers. Since a volunteer offers their service without pay, we must always let them know that they are *appreciated*. They give of their valuable time (away from family and usually after a full day at work) to be at rehearsals, performances and to prepare and practice their part on their own. Therefore, we should be respectful of the time they spend with us by starting rehearsals on time and ending them on time, too!

Burnout is likely for team members if we over-schedule them for too many services or special programs, without a sufficient period of rest between activities.

Consider the Cost

It's important to consider the *cost* of a performance or a special program in terms of human *and* financial resources. We must ask: How much time and effort is this going to require of our volunteers (are we taking away from our weekly "people budget" to make this happen)? Will the results of this event be worth the sacrifice of volunteer time and talent? Will it siphon away precious resources that will compromise the excellence expected in our weekly services?

Too many ministries misuse volunteers. We must make a conscious effort to not only *say* that we appreciate them, but also to *show* them that we respect their investment of time, heart and energy. Even a small gift like an occasional gift card will go a long way in saying "thank you!"

Everyone wants to be part of a success. Volunteers will go *way* beyond what's expected because they are proud to be on a winning team. Excellence, good leadership (spiritually, musically and organizationally), and a growing team are all attractive to prospective members. Leaders must find the right balance for volunteers, and to make sure that the ministry is ultimately about loving God *and* loving people.

Paying Musicians to Play

There are some instances where churches will pay musicians to play during a worship service or a special program. Some churches make it a

Worship Foundry

standard practice to pay each musician and singer weekly for every service. Obviously, this can be very expensive. Most congregations will never know who on the worship team is paid and who isn't. So when a paid person is brought on the team to play consistently, it's important that they fulfill the same spiritual and personal requirements as the volunteers. But in some cases, though, when hiring large groups of contracted musicians for special programs—string and horn sections, for instance—it can be difficult to find only Christian players. So if you are hiring a contractor to bring in outside players, it's wise to let them know what behavior is expected from everyone.

Some churches hire regulars who are non-believers, hoping that one day they'll choose to be Christ-followers. But in my opinion, a decision for Christ rarely happens in such cases. It's powerful to link God-loving, whole-hearted worshippers together to sing and play for the Lord. I've found that the imperfect offering of a sold-out heart for God is far more pleasing to the Lord than a stage full of non-Christian, professional musicians with excellent technical abilities, but who are tone-deaf to the Holy Spirit.

—SAMPLE—
Community Church Worship Ministry Membership Agreement 2020-21

Community Church **Mission**:

"To be a Spirit-led fellowship that worships God, shares the Good News of Christ, equips believers, and meets the needs of a growing community and changing world."

Community Church Worship Ministry **Purpose**:

To Exalt God by

1. Loving Him through personal, daily two-way communication (personal time of worship)
2. Fulfilling the priority of worship and allowing the world to witness the hope of Christ that is in us (corporate time of worship)

Jamie Harvill

To Edify the Body of Christ by:

1. Accompanying in worship
2. Promoting the priority of worship
3. Training new generations in the worship arts

To Evangelize the Lost

Community Church Worship Ministry <u>Vision</u>:
Provide teaching on subjects during rehearsal

2020: Making Jesus Our Pure and Holy Passion (Fall Worship Ministry Semester)

2021: Offering Our Lives to Serve God and Others (Spring Worship Ministry Semester)

Team Membership

- Each member must be a Christ-follower who exhibits continual spiritual growth and maturity
- Each member is expected to prepare for rehearsals and planned events by: Learning and rehearsing songs with the materials provided by the worship leader on Planning Center Online. Members are required to print their own charts for rehearsals and performances
- Each member must attend all scheduled rehearsals (except when sick or in the event of an emergency, and with proper notification). They must be ready and in place to start on time. Members understand, "no rehearsal, no performance"
- Each member is to act in a professional, adult manner, with a servant's attitude, commensurate with Christian principles, and are subject to dismissal from the team if warranted
- Each member is responsible for their own musical equipment, and the church will not be held responsible for lost or stolen items. It is recommended that each instrument or piece of personal equipment be insured through a personal homeowner's/ renter's insurance policy

Worship Foundry

- Each member must complete the term of one year on the worship team, at which time a recommitment will be required to continue for the next term
- Members who confirm an invitation for a particular week on Planning Center Online are required to inform the Worship Leader one week in advance of an absence (emergencies or illness are exceptions)
- Each member may be subject to a personal background check if asked to work in close proximity to children under the age of 18 during rehearsals and performances

Worship Leader (WL)

- The WL is to uphold the mission and vision of the church, as well as the worship ministry
- The WL is accountable to the pastor and the pastoral staff of the church
- The WL is responsible for the musical development of the worship and arts ministry
- The WL will choose all music, styles and presentations. Songs, productions and materials are at their discretion
- The WL will make decisions based upon the leadership of the Holy Spirit and in the council of the pastoral staff
- The WL is responsible for the spiritual development and care of each member under the senior pastor, and will prioritize spiritual development over musical involvement and development
- The WL reserves the right to choose assistants from within the team to help in developing and leading the worship ministry, based on musical ability, spiritual maturity and leadership qualities
- Any absences by the WL will be notified one week in advance, with the exception of illness or an emergency
- The WL has the flexibility to coordinate special rehearsals and to reschedule weekly rehearsals in order to accommodate substitute musicians/ singers, guest worship leaders and special services
- The WL will coordinate all weekly and special services as to songs, general program format, flow, and audio/visual production in cooperation with the pastoral staff

Jamie Harvill

- The WL will make available an order of service to each participating member through Planning Center Online for each regular and/ or special service

Worship Leadership Team

Chosen by and accountable to the Worship Leader

Associate Worship Leader:
Leads worship while WL is away; creates program lists and program format, approved by the WL, using the approved song list along with the support of the band and vocal leaders; generally assists WL in weekly worship ministry duties.

Band Leader/ Key Instrumentalist:
Leads band and may be called upon to be the designated leader when the WL is away. Has the authority to make musical changes and is in charge of band rehearsals when WL is away; may be called to lead other rehearsals outside of regular rehearsal; will consult with the Associate Worship Leader and Vocal Section Leader as to song lists and programs.

Vocal Leader:
Leads vocal section and may be called upon to be the designated leader when the WL is away. Has the authority to make musical changes and is in charge of vocal rehearsals when WL is away; may be called to lead other rehearsals outside of regular rehearsal; will consult with the Associate Worship Leader and Band Leader as to song list lists and programs.

Audio/ Visual Team Leader:
Leads the video, audio, computer, TV and lighting personnel; coordinates weekly A/V needs under the

direction of the WL. Helps recruit, train and schedule technical personnel for each service. Helps keep track of repairs, equipment needs/ changes and supplies. Has authority to adjust volume levels during services and special programs along with the pastoral staff. Any pastoral staff request for change of volume level is superior to any other.

Worship IT Manager:
Helps coordinate all matters regarding the development and management of Worship Ministry's website, under the direction of the WL.

Drama Team Leader:
Leads drama team and develops, rehearses and plans for performances in coordination with the WL; may be called upon to be the designated leader when the WL is away. Has the authority to make program changes; may be called to lead other rehearsals outside of regular rehearsal; will consult with the Associate Worship Leader and Band Leader as to song lists and programs.

Promotions Team Leader:
The Promotions Team Leader handles all written, A/V and print materials pertaining to promotion for Worship Ministry events and programs in cooperation with the WL; will be responsible for copywriting, editing, training, and website content.

Ministry/Hospitality Team Leader:
The Ministry/Hospitality Team Leader coordinates meals and worship ministry prayer concerns for members of the worship ministry; will coordinate hospitality for worship ministry functions, including backstage catering and the coffee/ snack table for pre-service and between services in the Green Room.

Jamie Harvill

I understand and prayerfully accept this agreement by signing my name below:

Worship Pastor:_____

Signature   Date

Member:_____

Signature   Date

Worship Ministry Questionnaire

Name:

Date:

Age: Gender: Married:

Children:

Name of Spouse

Regular attendee of Community Church?   Small Group?

Address:

City:

Zip:

Occupation: Cell: Home:

Email:

How do you prefer to receive correspondence? (circle) Email Mail Phone

What area of ministry do you wish to serve (circle)?

Choir   Vocal Team   Band   Tech Team

Orchestra   Dance Team   Drama Team

Do you have training and/or experience in the area you wish to serve?

Explain:

Vocal Experience? Explain below:

Vocal Range: S A T B

Instrumental Experience? Explain below:

Worship Foundry

Instrument (s)z:
Tech Experience? Explain:

Dance/Drama Experience? Explain:

Give a brief overview of your spiritual journey:

Vocal Audition Score Card

Judge:
Name:
Range: Date:
Choose a number between 1 and 10 (1=Poor—10=Excellent)
Pitch Accuracy- 1 2 3 4 5 6 7 8 9 10:
Vocal Quality/Tone- 1 2 3 4 5 6 7 8 9 10:
Recommended as soloist?
Ability to find part /chord changes- 1 2 3 4 5 6 7 8 9 10:
Appearance- 1 2 3 4 5 6 7 8 9 10:
Stage Presence- 1 2 3 4 5 6 7 8 9 10:
Recommendation:

Band Audition Score Card

Judge:
Name:
Instrument: Date:
Choose a number between 1 and 10 (1=Poor—10=Excellent)
Read Music Chart- 1 2 3 4 5 6 7 8 9 10:
Instrumental Ability/Tone- 1 2 3 4 5 6 7 8 9 10:
Ability To Find Part/Play With Others- 1 2 3 4 5 6 7 8 9 10:
Appearance- 1 2 3 4 5 6 7 8 9 10:
Stage Presence- 1 2 3 4 5 6 7 8 9 10:
Ability to solo:
Recommendation:

SECTION 4:
PLANNING AND PREPARATION

14. LIFE LESSONS FROM THE ROAD (MY PERSONAL JOURNEY)

My earliest experience in performing was playing guitar and singing in church plays and school talent shows. In my teens I even made a few bucks playing in dance bands with names like *Arabesque* and *Dark Star*. When I became a Christian, I played with local groups like *Homeward Bound* and *Luke Luker and the New Life Gospel Singers*. Although we spent more time practicing in someone's garage than playing gigs, the experience I gained helped build a foundation that would prepare me for the phone call I would receive in early 1980 from *American Entertainment Productions (AEP)*.

AEP was a small company situated in the northern suburbs of Columbus, Ohio. It might have been a tiny blip on the radar-screen of the entertainment industry, but it has been a "performance school" for many college-aged musicians and singers since 1973.

Wes Turner, the company's talent coordinator at the time, had received a recommendation that I audition as a guitar player for one of their touring groups. At the time of the call I was making plans to take a job driving a school bus, after poor grades discouraged me from continuing on to my second year of college. Needless to say, I was intrigued with the offer. Wes Turner was very convincing, too. He said that the group would be playing Top 40 music for junior and senior high school assemblies, and that we'd also be playing show music for corporate conventions in the evenings. Additionally, there was an upcoming USO tour to Germany and Iceland

Jamie Harvill

on the books for the spring. What bored and frustrated 19-year-old would balk at that opportunity?

Though extremely excited, I was also filled with anxiety, thinking about leaving home for the first time, setting off in a van full of strangers, and traveling to places I had only heard about in history books and geography class. I was a homebody, but also a dreamer, and I couldn't turn down this extraordinary proposition. After passing the audition, I bought my plane ticket, shopped for new clothes, and headed off into the wild blue yonder.

Wes first called me on a Friday morning and by Sunday night I was standing in the baggage claim area of the Toledo Airport, waiting for the group to pick me up. When I stepped onto that van as the newest member of the group *Life*, my life truly changed forever.

For the next three years I learned how to be an entertainer. I studied the art and skill of capturing, keeping and bringing joy to an audience— in any setting, indoors or out—rain or shine. By sheer necessity, I even learned how to sleep for 8-hours straight while sitting upright in a cramped passenger van.

My tenure with *AEP* took me all over the world; I played for a U.S. President, various politicians and Fortune-500 CEOs. We opened for world-famous singers and comedians in Las Vegas casinos and big-city theaters, spent a summer playing in Disney World, made the county fair circuit across Canada, and carried gear over garbage-filled loading docks, through slippery kitchens, and into hotel ballrooms—way too many to count. By the time January of 1983 rolled around, I was a seasoned performer and an experienced road manager who could deal with promoters, get a band to every gig, and faithfully practiced the motto: "The show must go on!"

I became a world-traveler, and *my* world became bigger in the process.

I consider the *AEP* experience to be my "secular" training, but God also had another opportunity for me that would prove to be my "sacred" training. In January of 1983, I received a call from Greg Golden in Mobile, Alabama.

Greg had called to ask me to audition. The audition led to a two-and-a-half-year stint with the group *Truth*. The group's founder and leader was Roger Breland. Roger was loved by his audiences: he had an incredible gift for weaving funny stories and tender spiritual moments together. He always delivered and is *still* a great entertainer.

Truth, for the span of 30 years—and before Roger retired the group in 2001—did almost 10,000 concerts, recorded 50 albums, traveled to more

Worship Foundry

than two dozen countries, and has performed to a combined audience of more than 10 million people. Truth's success was based largely on Roger—Mr. B as we called him—and his ability to recognize a great "moment."

I observed how Roger eased audiences into the palm of his hand every night during my tenure with *Truth.* I am still using some of those techniques I learned way back in 1983-85. I gleaned invaluable experience playing to secular audiences while traveling with *AEP,* too. These performance and ministry "schools" were a benefit to me, even today, as I plan and prepare worship services. An effective worship service contains many of the same ingredients and techniques as a secular performance. The difference, though, is that in worship the congregation becomes the lead singer and God is the audience!

15 The Concept of "Flow"

Back in 1997, while on an American Airlines flight high above the Midwest, I ran across an article in *Wired Magazine* by John Geirland entitled, "Go with the Flow." It illustrated how a person can be engaged and effectively drawn into the experience of surfing the web. Geirland interviewed renowned psychologist and educator, Mihaly Csikszentmihalyi (pronounced: me-HIGH chick-sent-me-HIGH-ee—I'll refer to him as "MC"), who created the *Theory of Flow* in the 1970s, while attempting to develop a better understanding of human behavior as it relates to happiness and contentment.

In the *Wired* interview, MC described the *state of flow* as: "[When] the ego falls away. Time flies. Every action, movement, and thought follows inevitably from the previous one, like playing jazz. Your whole being is involved..." I was intrigued with how this theory not only applies to the experience of surfing the web, but can also be of help when planning worship services.

As stated in another chapter, to entertain is to *maintain* one's emotional sensation or a state of mind. Amusement plays an important part in entertainment, and the process of maintaining one's attention is made possible through *uninterrupted flow*.

When we apply the *theory of flow* to our worship services, we employ communication techniques that skilled story tellers have used throughout history. These techniques help draw the attention of the congregation into the worship experience and maintain their full and active participation. *Flow* remains consistent when the congregation is comfortable in their

Jamie Harvill

environment: when they're not hungry, too hot or too cold—when the seating is comfortable, and the lighting and sound are set just right.

Jesus was careful to meet the basic needs of His audience before preaching His sermons. On one such occasion, Jesus needed to get away and spend some time alone. Upon returning, He stepped off His boat into a huge gathering of more than 5,000 people waiting on the shore. Our story picks up in the fourteenth verse of Matthew, chapter 14:

> *"When Jesus landed and saw a large crowd, he had compassion on them and healed their sick. As evening approached, the disciples came to him and said, 'This is a remote place, and it's already getting late. Send the crowds away, so they can go to the villages and buy themselves some food.' Jesus replied, 'They do not need to go away. You give them something to eat.' 'We have here only five loaves of bread and two fish,' they answered. 'Bring them here to me,' he said. And he directed the people to sit down on the grass. Taking the five loaves and the two fish and looking up to heaven, he gave thanks and broke the loaves. Then he gave them to the people. They all ate and were satisfied, and the disciples picked up twelve basketfuls of broken pieces that were left over. The number of those who ate was about five thousand men, besides women and children. (verses 14-21)"*

We see that Jesus' first order of business was to meet the immediate physical needs of the crowd: He healed the sick. Then, as the sun was setting after a long day of ministry, Jesus knew the crowd was hungry, tired and needed a break. He directed them to sit on a cool, comfortable grassy area, and made provision to feed every man, woman and child present.

The same incident is recorded in John chapter 6. After the miraculous feast of bread and fish, Jesus slipped away again. The next morning, crowds went searching for Him. When they found Him on the other side of the lake, Jesus took the opportunity to explain that *He* is the bread of life from heaven. He used the miracle from the day before to illustrate that *He* was spiritual food, and that they must allow *Him* into their lives to be truly satisfied. He wanted them to know the *deeper* spiritual meaning of the miracles He performed, and it was important to first take care of their physical needs before meeting their spiritual need.

Worship Foundry

A little recap of Jesus' hillside miracle feast:

- He healed the sick
- He gave them a comfortable place to sit
- He fed them until they were satisfied
- He let them get a full night's rest
- Then He taught them about the Manna from Heaven

Jesus knows that our needs and human limitations are the same in the 21st century.

The people to which we minister on a weekly basis have a limited attention span; their inability to sit or stand for a lengthy amount of time—without a bathroom break—will scream for their attention much louder than the message we want to deliver. When the physical needs of the audience go unattended, they *will* be distracted.

Jesus knew how to tell stories, and how to relate to the audience through the use of parables. In this way, the listeners—with the help of the Holy Spirit—were able to glean truth from His amazing stories. Therefore, using Jesus as our example of how to communicate, the content and structure of our services must be scrutinized for *clarity* and *relevance*, and the overall message must be *applicable*. We must use this same scrutiny even when choosing music.

Before we even set pencil to paper regarding our weekend service plans though, we need to consider the *physical needs of our audience*: Are they comfortable (temperature, seating, sight-line to the stage)? Is the volume of the music and preaching too loud or soft? Are the songs in keys that are congregation-friendly, with lyrics that are easy to sing and easy to read on the screens? Is the lighting adequate? Is the facility (size, structure, amenities, etc.) able to meet the needs of our congregation? Is every physical aspect of our facility—from the parking lot to the entrance of the building, through the hallways, childcare areas, classrooms, restrooms, and into our auditorium— a help or a hindrance in delivering the message?

We must also pay close attention to the *emotional aspects of our services and facilities*, so that our visitors and regular attenders feel anticipated, welcomed, honored and cared-for—that they have an opportunity to connect with others in a safe and comfortable atmosphere, and in a positive, loving environment, where both young and old, singles and families, can flourish spiritually.

Jamie Harvill

Remove the Stones

In Isaiah, chapters 40-66, we read of the Babylonian captivity, and subsequently of the Jewish exiles' return to Jerusalem. It was proclaimed:

> *"Pass through, pass through the gates! Prepare the way for the people. Build up, build up the highway! Remove the stones. Raise a banner for the nations" (Isaiah 62:10).*

The way of their return needed to be cleared of all obstructions. *John Wesley's Explanatory Notes* breaks this verse down to its nuts and bolts in 18th-century English:

- **Go through** [pass through]— is doubled by way of emphasis. Go meet the Gentiles, whom God purposes to bring into the church.
- **Prepare**— let them not have any obstructions in their way.
- **Stones**— that there be no stumbling-stone, or [offense] in their way.
- **Standard** [banner]— an allusion to soldiers, that set up their standard that the army may know where to repair from all quarters [to return from every direction].

In other words: *Let the people clearly see the Lord, high and lifted up, with nothing in their path to stop them from running to His throne of grace. Let the flag of His salvation fly high for all to see! Let everyone gather to worship Him!*

As facilitators of worship, we are encouraged to clear away modern-day distractions that inhibit people from experiencing and drawing near to the Risen Lord. Here are a few basic, inexpensive, first-step solutions for any church that desires to improve their worship environment:

1. Maintain a pleasing stage area (hide wires, remove trash and clutter, etc.)
2. Maintain a comfortable room temperature
3. Maintain clean, modest and attractive attire on stage
4. Provide clean, safe and secure nursery and childcare facilities (nothing ruins a service for a mother more than feeling unsure of their child's welfare)

Worship Foundry

5. Make use of greeters, ushers and other worship hosts to help create a pleasant, personal and positive experience for regular attendees and visitors (they can also assist if there's a medical emergency in the congregation, if any security issues arise, or to help anticipate and diffuse any other distractions while the pastoral staff keeps their focus on the needs of the service)
6. Maintain clean and well-composed restroom facilities, classrooms and hallways
7. Provide ample and clear signage inside and outside the facilities to provide directions to all areas of the church
8. Place worship hosts throughout the facility (not just the entrances) who actively seek out guests to greet, answer questions, and to help point them (or walk with them) to where they need to go
9. Set up a highly-visible information station staffed with worship hosts as a touch point for questions about the church, information about small groups, sign-ups, event information, etc.

In time, a church must invest in a suitable sound, video and lighting system commensurate with the layout of the worship space, their musical needs, congregation size, and anticipated growth of the congregation.

The Ultimate Goal of the Service

The ultimate goal in our services is to help facilitate a *One-on-one encounter between the participant and God.* When planning, it's important to analyze every aspect of the service to make sure that each component is effective in reaching the objective.

The stage may be wonderfully decorated and lit, with the best performers available and the greatest songs; the sound system may be state-of-the-art, with a stellar high-definition video system. But if we haven't thought through and carefully planned how people are to move on stage—how each component in the program properly fits together—we'll end up looking like the Keystone Cops, bumbling around on stage!

Therefore, we must design seamless interplay between each segment of the service, so that the audience will find it easier to maintain an *uninterrupted focus and attention* on the message we've planned for them to experience.

Spend time with your production team to see that every detail is in place. Make sure to clearly communicate the "Big Idea" of the service—the theme, the take-away, the challenge. Take time in the days following the service to discuss which aspects succeeded, which failed, and how to make improvements. And don't forget, it's important to celebrate, too.

Jamie Harvill

Here are some basic suggestions for creating a seamless flow on stage:

- **Plan stage moves**-Plan and rehearse in advance the stage moves involved in each service (how and when each person or item comes on and off stage). Avoid "dead-air space" by making sure each participant on stage knows how and to whom they will "hand off" their segment. Talk through stage moves in the planning meeting, then again before the service

- **Confirm proper flow between segments**-When making transitions, try to match the *emotion* from the preceding segment in order to create an appropriate, seamless transition into the following segment (i.e., worship into announcements; prayer into closing, etc.). Decide what you are going to say in advance. Knee-jerk transitions are flow-killers

- **Test the equipment**- Check that *each piece of equipment* used in the service is working before the service begins; don't assume

- **Protect the pulpit**-The pulpit area is the most visible place in the auditorium. Therefore, with respect to its importance, the pulpit must be reserved for those who are equipped to speak from the microphone. Make sure to coach whoever stands at the pulpit to speak clearly and into the microphone, to know what they are going to say, and to save spontaneity for those with more experience. As said in a preceding chapter, avoid the temptation to open up the pulpit indiscriminately to anyone, because unfortunate results cause the congregation to feel "held captive," and this can destroy an otherwise pleasant experience as well as any trust in the future.

• • •

An effective worship service that flows, amuses, enlightens, inspires and motivates people to move toward God requires much planning. We must be guided in the whole process by the Holy Spirit, then submit our plans and the outcome to God, Who is in control. Be willing to make changes and adjustments as the Spirit leads.

Worship Foundry

Leaders are facilitators in the congregation's worship journey; they can make or break a service by not paying close attention to details. Once the physical, environmental and emotional obstacles are removed, the congregation can more easily flow into worship. Again, the ultimate goal in our services is to facilitate a *One-on-one encounter between the participant and God.*

Rehearsal Preparation

It's a common problem that team members come to rehearsal unprepared. Is this because *you* are unprepared as their leader? Did you give your team sufficient time to study their parts before rehearsal, or throw together a plan at the last minute? If being unprepared is a habit of yours, then it's no wonder you have a difficult time recruiting people for your worship team, that the services aren't bringing the results you want, and the quality of production is poor. *Great services start with a well designed plan and an effective rehearsal.*

An effective rehearsal helps the team to be musically, mentally, technically and spiritually ready by service time. It takes plenty of time to design the service, collect resources, build support media, and arrange and distribute music before rehearsal. For some churches with complex production requirements, it may require 6-8 weeks to prepare all of the components of the service. The more complicated a church's production needs, the farther out a team must begin planning. Every church must find its own prep-time requirement. My suggestion is for the smallest church, with the least number of production components, to have a completed set list at least **2 weeks in advance** of a service (more time may be needed for special programs).

Excellence is not for the timid, lazy, or the faint of heart. In order for goals to be accomplished, a leader must get ahead of the team to help them prepare for success. If one is not willing to do so, then leadership is in serious question.

Jamie Harvill

Pre-Rehearsal Tech and Resource Preparation

Thank God for our tech crews! They can make or break us. Proper communication with them is essential. Give the tech crew a cue list far enough in advance so they will be ready for rehearsal. They need to know who is going to sing a solo, speak, announce, etc., so they can set up microphones and program the mixer (digital boards), set lighting instruments and program the lighting console. It's helpful when the sound person running the mixer on the weekend is at the rehearsal and can practice the cues themselves.

Whichever method you use to distribute materials in advance of rehearsal, be it electronic or otherwise, make sure you include a worship song list, music charts, lyrics, and recorded demos of the songs that convey the way you generally want them to sound. I currently use *Planning Center Online* because it's a well-organized, one-stop-shop for posting service resources, scheduling team members, and much more.

Make sure that your team members have the tools they need to succeed. The arrangements, keys and tempos from the demo mp3s may be different than what you will eventually perform, but the demos should be sufficient to help the band and singers initially find their parts. Matching the charts to the mp3 demos is a huge help, with the understanding that the roadmap (Verse, Chorus, Bridge, etc.) may differ. To distribute these items in a legal manner, you must acquire licensing from *CCLI* or my friends at *Christian Copyright Solutions*.

It's imperative that leaders make decisions regarding flow, segues, instrumentation, vocal parts, stage moves, etc., before rehearsal. If it can be decided beforehand, then settle it! Leave as few unanswered questions as possible.

• • •

Leaders must come to each rehearsal with a plan to hit every area of need for the upcoming service. It is important to put a time limit on weekly rehearsals. I recommend no more than *90 minutes*. Special productions such as Christmas, Easter, etc., may require more time.

Take time to tidy up the rehearsal space before practice. Discard clutter and straighten wires to create a clean, stress-free environment, and to promote peace and creativity

Worship Foundry

If you need help in making musical decisions, have a discussion with a skilled musician on your team before rehearsal to help you implement your ideas. Some leaders may have less ability to communicate technical and musical directions than others. If you make your decisions about arrangements in advance, and map out the transitional points in a set list before rehearsal, you can more effectively focus time on the challenging passages and spend less time with the easier ones. Plan to hit the more challenging sections a couple of times.

In short, to prepare for rehearsal an effective leader must:

- Purpose to prepare services *at least* 2 weeks in advance
- Distribute rehearsal resources in a timely, legal and effective manner
- Create a rehearsal game-plan that can be accomplished within *90 minutes*
- Create musical alliances on your team to give technical, musical and personal support
- Clean up rehearsal space clutter to start fresh each week
- Give the tech crew a "heads up" for what you might need in the way of support prior to rehearsal
- Be the strong leader that your church and your team needs!

Your commitment to excellence, and the success that follows, will help attract people to the Kingdom and to your team, and will bring personal reward and satisfaction to you and your volunteers.

Chord Charts and Lead Sheets

One area of debate among worship team members and leaders is which system of musical communication is most effective. Leaders tend to stay within their own comfort zones, and usually supply the team with their preferred system. The three most common are: *chord-over-word-style sheets*, *lead sheet/charts* and the *Nashville Number System*.

Frankly, I use each of these methods at certain times, and I especially make use of the Nashville Number System while writing, figuring out chords to a new song, or creating an arrangement. But I prefer to use detailed charts which I create myself in *Finale®*, or charts purchased from resources like *Praise Charts*.

Below is a quick description of each system, along with their pros and cons. I'm sure that proponents of any particular system will want to staunchly defend its use. I understand. Musicians are passionate, and the debate over written forms of music continues to stir up heated conversation!

Chord-Over-Word Sheets

This system is the most common among guitar-based worship teams. With the words written out and chords situated directly above, each player can easily reference a song's structure with little difficulty. It's easy for someone with limited musical training to create their own arrangements and use this system.

Jamie Harvill

The Pros:

- Chords-over-words charts are easy to read and write (no music reading skills necessary)
- Most songs can be typed or written out in their entirety on a single sheet of paper
- The song's layout (roadmap) can be written in shorthand at the top of the page
- They are a good, quick reference guide to the song during performance

The Cons:

- Chords-over-words charts don't accurately include time durations between chord changes
- They don't offer intricate details of rhythm, dynamic expression, written melodies or specific instrumental cues
- Chords must be rewritten if a key change is necessary
- They are not an effective detailed representation of a song, especially when cataloging and creating a formal library of worship music

<u>Charts</u>

As charts and lead sheets utilize formal musical notation, they take some skill to read and compose. By nature, though, this system proves to be the most comprehensive of all three systems mentioned for use of its specific musical information.

It's up to the writer of each chart to determine just how much "detail" is necessary for a song. For practical means, the arranger may want to limit information on the chart in order to cut down on the amount of page turns. Typically, a lead sheet will include the melody and lyrics of a song, but sometimes a basic chord chart is all that is necessary to document chord changes with rhythms and durations, the roadmap, dynamics and expression. I prefer to limit charts to two pages, if possible.

Even though a worship team doesn't require a detailed lead sheet all of the time, it's good to have a written melody available for reference purposes. A chord chart will usually suffice on a weekly basis.

Worship Foundry

The Pros:
- Charts offer a comprehensive, detailed representation of a song
- If composed with a software program like *Finale®*, a song's key can be quickly and easily transposed on the fly; several songs can be put together by using the program's cut and paste feature to fuse different documents into one single chart
- Instrumental cues can be documented and written out for quick reference
- The proper lyric and melody can be notated together on the chart
- Everyone on the team can reference the song, including sections and measure numbers
- A single *master chart* is used for each song during rehearsal and performance, representing the "DNA" of the song

The Cons:
- Charts take some musical training to read and compose
- Notation software is expensive and involves a significant amount of time and effort to learn
- Many songs require more than one page
- They are difficult for worship leaders to use during performance

Nashville Number System

This system was developed in the 1950s by Nashville session singer and member of the famed *Jordanaires*, Neal Matthews, Jr. It was further developed by multi-instrumental session wiz, Charlie McCoy. The simple system replaces letter symbols for numbers when referring to chords in a song. In the key of *G*, for instance, the seven chords of the basic progression are:

G (1)　**Am** (2m)　**Bm** (3m)　**C** (4)　**D** (5)　**Em** (6m)　**F#dim**(7dim)

Most chord progressions in country and pop-styles of music use a variation of the above sequence. Outside of using differing keys, most songs contain similar chord patterns.

Take the common chord progression of **G** to **C** to **D**. By referring to the corresponding numbers next to the letters in the above diagram, the progression can also be written: **1** to **4** to **5**. In the case of number

Jamie Harvill

system creator Neal Matthews, Jr., it was often necessary to change keys on the fly to suit the singer during a recording session. Instead of re-writing the charts, and using letters for chord symbols, the leader would provide number charts, making it easier, if necessary, to transpose to any key. That way, the chord progression of **1** to **4** to **5** in the key of **A**, is the equivalent of **A** to **D** to **E**; or in the key of **D**: **D** to **G** to **A**, and so forth.

Many churches outside of Nashville are now using this method to chart out songs for the worship band. The numbers can easily be called out in groupings of four measures; in a short period of time, a band leader can call out an entire song.

There is no formal system of writing out Nashville numbers, but each player sticks to a few rules that keep the system organized on one page. It's a great system to use as a quick reference.

The Pros:
- The Nashville Number System is a great system for calling out chords for a new song
- One song can be contained on a single sheet of paper
- It's ideal for making key changes
- It's useful for quickly jotting down chords from a recording

The Cons
- The Nashville Number System takes effort to mentally transpose from key to key
- Rhythmic notation is limited in the system, although there are some basic shortcuts to symbolize "pushed" eighth-notes and whole-note "diamonds," for instance
- Chords outside of the seven numbers represented in the basic system can prove to be challenging, especially on-the-fly, (**flat-6** and **flat-7**, for example)
- Like the chord-over-word charts, it's not the most effective detailed representation of a song, especially for the purpose of cataloging and creating a formal library of worship music

Worship Foundry

A Beautiful Sculptured Image

Regarding the importance of creating detailed documents of songs, I recently came across an interesting passage. In the book, *Behind The Boards: The Making of Rock 'n' Roll's Greatest Records Revealed*, author Jake Brown interviews famed record producer Daniel Lanois about his work with the Irish mega-group, *U2*.

Brown asks what Lanois considers to be an important tool as a music producer. "Note-taking," he answers. In the interview, Lanois explains that he documents each recording session in great detail with notes on instruments used in a particular song, along with effects, EQ, compressor and fader markings, etc.

For each song, Lanois prefers "writing out an arrangement, which is a very big part of what I do. I use graph paper for that; sometimes I use very big books, like a 12 x 18 graph page, and I start on the left and right of the pad—the long part which is horizontal—and I just write out the arrangement, and everything gets included on that page: all lyrics, all tempo shifts, all rises and falls and dynamics, notations about what needs to be reminded of at the next meeting. So by this one page, you see a complete graphic display of the song—the way it's structured. So when you get in the band room, you can speak and connect it well because you know what you're talking about relative to a beautiful sculptured image."

Getting On the the Same Page

Like Lanois, I prefer to have an overall view of the song stretched out before me. When I lead worship, though, I must do some memorization, since, in my opinion, having a music stand between me and the audience can be a bit cumbersome and distracting. In a situation where I'll need to reference a chart while leading worship, I attach my iPad to the mic stand at a low enough level so that it's not a distraction, and I connect a Bluetooth pedal to turn pages while I play.

If I am playing guitar, but not on the front line, I use my iPad, loaded with the master chord charts for the service.

I find it frustrating when a band reads from different charts for the same song. The point of a good chart is to bring everyone together on common ground. In some cases, it's necessary for drummers to create a

Jamie Harvill

more manageable chart to reduce page-turning while playing. When doing this, it's always best to refer to the master chart and make notes to match sections and measures. That way, the band leader can address things at specific places from the master chart.

To introduce the more sophisticated chart system to your team, it will require training, patience and discipline. Plus, it will require commitment of both time and resources to create charts yourself, or by someone else on your team. *Praise Charts* is an excellent resource for supplying sheet music for your favorite worship songs if you aren't able to commit to doing your own custom charts.

Ways to get on the same page:

- Don't simply rely on chords-over-word sheets; make the transition to chord charts and lead sheets
- Offer training for a team member, or learn how to use notation software yourself in order to make custom charts for your team
- Offer musical training for those who cannot read music. At the very least, train your team how to read rhythms and chord changes on a staff
- Many popular songs have several versions, so clearly list the name of the artist and the CD on the chart from which the recording originates, along with other corresponding resources
- Encourage players to use master charts for songs in rehearsal, and discard outdated resources attached to songs that don't match the master chart and recording (this includes lyrics)
- Use a great service like *Planning Center Online*, a place to store and display all of your resources in one convenient location
- Go to the next level with your team. Pursue excellence!

Number charts are especially handy in the short term for sketching out a quick arrangement; I use this method frequently. But I must emphasize the importance of using charts in the long run.

There are times when it's impossible to fully memorize each part for every song in a set. Sometimes I'm handed a song I've never seen or played before. Taking a moment to scan each page, I make notes, highlight the repeats, endings and codas, etc., and then jump in with both feet. It doesn't mean I play it perfectly the first time, but I can more confidently approach

Worship Foundry

unfamiliar songs when I use charts. When songs contain a number of difficult chord changes, charts become necessary. Also, when I'm invited to play guitar at another church, and the song arrangements are unfamiliar, I've learned to trust the chart, and not my memory.

Creating literate music teams in our churches will bring significant dividends. Not only will the team grow musically—with the ability to do a variety of musical styles—but their value as players will grow exponentially as well. If we teach our up-and-coming players how to read music, we can have the satisfaction of knowing that we've trained a new generation of musicians who can jump into most any musical situation and succeed. What happened to the days when the church was the world-leader in the arts? We can get back to educating young people, and sending out the world's finest musicians *from our local churches.*

Planning a Service

The 5 "Ss" of planning a service

1. Determine the Spiritual **Statement** of the service ("Big Idea," theme, takeaway)
2. Determine the **Song** Selection (Positional reference, tempo, key)
3. Determine the song **Sequence** (order of the songs and spoken segments)
4. Arrange the **Segues** (content which ties each piece together in the service)
5. Be **Sensitive** (to people and, more importantly, the Holy Spirit)

Spiritual Statement

Each church has a unique personality, and the songs used in that fellowship during worship contribute to the "DNA" of each congregation. Songs that are used week to week say a lot about a church: who they are, where they're going, what's important to them, and reveal a lot about their theology.

As one considers the songs for a given week, it's important to consider the *spiritual statement* to be made in a given service as a whole. This could relate to a certain series the pastor is teaching, or a special scripture or topic. It may be a seasonal theme or a special presentation that will determine how the service will be constructed or thematically framed.

Consider the congregation: is it of a certain age or will it consist of mixed generations? Some generations outside of the main demographic will probably feel left out at times, but the objective is to reach the *greatest population*. Some churches have different services with different styles of music, and that's up to each organization to determine.

Songs that fit together thematically help keep the topic focused. If the songs are carefully knit together into a flowing, prayer-like journey, where the worship leader becomes virtually invisible (always a good thing!), the congregation can enter into true worship and a One-on-one encounter with God. The more connectivity of songs in a selection—relating to the overall theme of the service—the less narrative is necessary on behalf of the worship leader. *Let the songs do the talking as much as possible!*

Song Selection

As previously mentioned, the choice of certain songs is unique to each congregation. There are no *right* or *wrong* songs to use—just *effective* ones—those that foster connection with God. Some songs are written **about** God, and are filled with statements about His character, majesty, holiness, etc. (many hymns are written about God). Other songs make statements **to** God, as if in a conversation.

Selecting the most effective songs can make or break the worship song set. Here's a scenario that you might have experienced from time to time:

It's Monday, and you look over your shoulder to the past weekend's services, making the observation that nobody sang along with you during the song set. It's so easy to blame the congregation—after all, the songs you chose were top-charting worship choruses and you even sprinkled in a few hymns. But they just stood there looking at you, arms folded, mute and seemingly disinterested. Of course it was the congregation's fault: they are spiritually immature and musically unsophisticated ...right?

Let's try to sort out some of the reasons that may have contributed to the "cricket-moment" Sunday. *First*, there are basic things to look for in the building blocks of a good congregational song:

- **The melody is easy to remember** the second time through; is user-friendly with intervals that are not difficult to reach (usually with no more than a leap of a perfect 5th— an interval of a major 7th is difficult for the average person to hear)

Worship Foundry

- **The lyrics are easy to sing, Biblically sound, culturally relevant and are universally understood** within the congregation (beware of theologically controversial concepts; words that take a dictionary to define)

- **The lyrics and melody are emotionally congruent,** and work together to create the desired mood for the moment

Second, if you've selected songs that contain the building blocks just mentioned, then here are some more considerations: Was the tempo too fast or slow? Was the key suitable for the congregation? Was a certain song a personal favorite, but maybe one the congregation didn't care for? Were there too many new songs introduced in one service?

The Positional Reference, Tempo and Key

- **Determine the "positional reference" of the song**

   Horizontal Songs
   Horizontal songs are ones where we sing **about** God in what English grammar refers to as "third person." Many hymns incorporate a horizontal focus, where we as the congregation voice truths about God: His character, holiness, righteousness, etc.

   Vertical Songs
   Vertical songs are ones where we sing directly **to** God in "second person," Such songs are more prayer-like or conversational in nature.

Choosing the most appropriate song for the moment is an art. Even though there is no "right way," I find that placing horizontal-type songs toward the beginning of a service helps the congregation to fix their minds and hearts on the attributes of God, on Who He is. It helps us draw near to an awesome, powerful and loving God. Then, using vertical-type songs when the service transitions into a more intimate setting, the lyrics become more prayerful, creating a One-on-one conversation.

I select individual songs that stick to one consistent *positional reference*

Jamie Harvill

point throughout the song (I am careful to write songs with this in mind, too). In other words, the "person" of a song (*to* God or *about* God) must remain consistent—in first-, second- or third-person, all the way through to the end. Songs that have *mixed positional references*, without proper orientation, will be confusing for the listener, and certainly for the congregation singing the song.

Determine the Tempo of a Song

The tempo of a song—whether fast, medium or slow—creates varying degrees of energy in a service. Faster songs with exciting lyrics help create a more enthusiastic emotion, helping to draw the congregation's attention away from themselves to focus toward the front of the room, and ultimately toward God.

Medium-tempo songs create a transition point in the service—they help smooth the journey between singing songs of an energetic group-perspective, into slow-tempo, contemplative-type songs where we offer personal prayers to God.

To find a suitable tempo for a song, locate the section of the song's lyric that has the most syllables—usually in the chorus of most songs. Sing the lyric and adjust the tempo to where it feels comfortable—not too rushed for fast songs, and not so slow that it seems to drag. Tempos that are too fast can create a frantic feel; ones that are too slow can create a lethargic feel. *Choosing the wrong tempo may be the reason your congregation won't sing along.*

An effective song set will feel like a complete journey, from a starting place of being "a single voice in a crowd," to then being "face to face with God" in worship. It takes sufficient *time* to lead our congregation to this place.

I find it difficult to start a service with a slow song (although it can be effective on occasion), because in most cases the audience has just come from their car or small group, or maybe they've just dropped their kids off at their Sunday school classrooms or the nursery. To jump right in to a solemn atmosphere, and to sing intimate worship songs to the Lord can be a difficult emotional transition, and most people need a chance to "warm up" to the worship environment...after all, we're human!

Worship Foundry

A journey has a beginning, middle and an end, so construct the service with this in mind. Think of how a great play or movie draws you in, helps you to forget about yourself, takes you through a variety of emotional spaces, to finally bring you to a tender finale. We must be conscious of how human emotions operate. Most people need to be *gently led* and not *violently dragged* into worship!

Determine the Key of A Song

The choice of key for a song is one of the factors that will determine whether or not your audience will sing with you. I can't say it enough: *In worship, the congregation is the <u>lead singer</u>.*

As worship leader, you are a facilitator in helping the congregation "win" in worship. We must find every opportunity to aid them in singing to God.

The problem with the congregation not participating may be with your choice of key. It's time to address this problem, one that seems to be increasingly prevalent in churches: people can't sing the songs in worship because they are in a key that is out of their *singing range*.

Most pop worship songs are recorded to promote the lead vocalist on the recording. The original recordings sound great with all of the high notes and all of the extras the singer puts into the performance. Sometimes we use the same key as the original recording because of our desire to capture the same energy and excitement of the recording in our services. It's also true that we choose keys to suit our own singing range and comfort zones.

I'll say it again: *The congregation is the lead singer.* In order for the congregation to comfortably sing along, we must consider the average range in which most people sing—it's significantly limited. Even though altering a song from its original key may be frustrating, arranging songs with the *congregational singing range* in mind is our highest priority when choosing keys for *congregational* songs. If you are doing a song in a service for special music, with a soloist in mind, by all means make the key suitable for their range. But when the *congregation* is the lead singer, make the key suitable for the *congregation* to sing.

The following diagram shows the *congregational singing range on a keyboard:*

Jamie Harvill

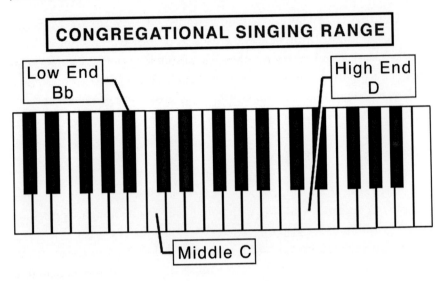

Tenor and soprano ranges fit comfortably within the *congregational singing range*. When *altos* and *baritones* choose song keys to fit their range, though, the melody is usually *too high* or *too low* for the average congregation.

The *congregational singing range* principle is also a helpful tool in writing songs: Don't go below the **Bb** (see diagram), or above a **D** in the melody, unless it's to reach a quick passing note that's no more than a whole-step away, and don't stay on those higher notes for very long. *As a worship leader, it's really about being a servant to our congregation and not about displaying our vocal abilities.*

Sequencing

The sequence represents the list of songs and how they work together. Like I said earlier, it's my preference to sequence the songs by placing the ones *about* God closer to the beginning of the service as the congregation is warming up to the room's atmosphere.

The mental picture here is much like inviting people to your home: you greet them at the door and work your way inside. Everyone settles in, becoming relaxed as the evening progresses. Conversations then become more personal as defenses fall and authentic communication begins.

Segues

Segues between songs and worship moments are critical. Try to allow as little lag-time between each piece as possible. Even nanoseconds of "dead air" are distracting to great worship moments.

Work out key changes by using the simple technique of going to the dominant chord of the new key, and using a suspended 4th in the first two beats of the bar, then resolving it on the last two beats. After that, you can land on the tonic or the "one chord" of the new key. Sometimes a "cold transition"—starting the new key with no modulation—will work just fine. It's all about the feel of the moment.

A tempo can also be changed by gradually slowing down (ritard) during the modulation. By keeping songs with related keys together, as well as modulating by half or whole steps, the outcome is a cleaner and better flowing transition.

It's okay to let the congregation take a moment to contemplate between songs. These are moments of planned silence, which the Psalms refer to as *Selah*, meaning to "ponder" or to "think on this for a moment."

Sensitivity

I try to be sensitive to those who are in the service each weekend. The emotions that flow from a personal connection with a song is important (like with hymns and songs that are an integral part of someone's beginning steps in a life-long spiritual journey). The *ultimate* goal, though, is for the congregation to *connect with God*. So in the planning stage I try to remove any distractions that may inhibit that connection (like we spoke of before in the Isaiah 62:10 passage)—be it *physical, emotional, musical,* or *spiritual*. I choose and arrange the songs with this in mind. Each stage movement must be scrutinized in order to uncover anything that may inhibit a full focus on God during worship.

The ultimate sensitivity and allegiance must be to God: He is the ultimate focal point and the object of our adoration. We must always be ready to make a change of plan when God leads us in another direction. Our plans are just a flexible starting-point in the greater scheme of things.

Pray before you prepare the service. Think about taking the congregation on a worship journey.

Jamie Harvill

• • •

Technology, the Jesus Movement, and the New Worship Order

Church music has made an astonishing transformation over the past fifty years. As I mentioned earlier when speaking of the "worship wars," this revolution's roots stretch back to the hippie days of the '60s and early '70s.

After becoming Christ followers, these counter-culture castaways began attending churches like Calvary Chapel Costa Mesa in California, writing their own praise songs, and forming Jesus-rock bands to spread the Gospel. *Maranatha! Music* then became the unofficial record company of the Jesus Movement on the west coast of the United States, and Chuck Smith from Calvary Chapel, along with a handful of others, became the de facto pastors of the movement.

Over the years, this phenomenon surged into a worship music tidal wave that eventually flooded the entire country. By the '80s, the deluge led to the creation of the out-of-the-mainstream, independent record company based in Mobile, Alabama: *Integrity Music.* They began their ascent by distributing tapes of new worship songs every six weeks to subscribers. In the decades since, worshipers have seen thousands of these new songs transform people and churches worldwide through *Integrity Music's* pop music-stylings, singable melodies and conversational lyrics.

The Long and Winding Road: The evolution of congregational singing

Congregational singing goes way back to the days of the early church, when liturgical texts were chanted. The Greek cultural influences of the time were borrowed and incorporated into songs of praise. Before the Reformation, congregational singing was not allowed by Catholic laypersons, but instead the liturgy was performed in Latin by the clergy.

The invention of the printing press led to a proliferation of hymnals, out of which percolated some 250 ubiquitous hymns that would eventually bare an ecclesiastical "thumbs up," deeming the selections proper for the flock. Congregations sang these songs in churches everywhere, and eventually everyone knew these hymns by heart. Then, as if slamming on a huge air brake—with the use of desktop computers in worship, and with advancements in projection—American churches all but ditched the hymnal, in trade for praise songs displayed on pull-down movie screens.

When thousands of pastors from various denominations began attending *Promise Keepers* rallies in the '90s, many who were skeptical about new, emerging worship choruses were eventually won-over by the power of experiencing heart-felt worship first-hand. As a result of this life-changing experience, many pastors began allowing guitars, drums and rock music styles into their services, in hopes of capturing the same emotional and spiritual results they witnessed at the rallies. In time, they either augmented the ever-present choir, or began to dismiss the large vocal ensemble altogether.

As a cumulative result, there has been a significant decline in the market of printed music for church choirs. On the other hand, though, as a result of this bourgeoning new music genre, mainline recording companies—known for promoting Christian performance artists—began marketing worship songs, performed by "worship artists," who then helped propel "Praise and Worship" into a steady upward trajectory.

Probably the most significant shift in worship music popularity happened when Michael W. Smith made his debut in this new Christian music sub-genre with his CD, *Worship*. It was fatefully released on September 11, 2001, and included such classics as "Open the Eyes of My Heart," "Forever," and "The Heart of Worship." Soon after, and probably due in part to a spiritual reaction to the 9/11 attacks, praise and worship started to become a popular radio format. Church goers were hearing songs on the radio, as were the worship leaders and music directors, and this led to a barrage of more worship songs being introduced to the church through radio. As a result, even more new songs continued to find their way into the church.

Since its launch in October of 1988, the copyright licensing organization, CCLI, has grown to represent 200,000 churches with its stated mission (from the website): "as a ministry of the Church and a service to the Church, to educate the Church about copyright laws, to protect the Church from the consequences of copyright infringements and to encourage greater utilization of copyrights in Church services." Through the services of CCLI, "The Church Copyright License is a contractual agreement with songwriters and publishers from around the world. For an annual license fee, a church receives legal authorization to copy from over 200,000 songs

Jamie Harvill

for congregational use." A popular CCLI song has the potential to generate handsome revenues for song writers and publishers. For song writers like me, CCLI provides a major portion of royalty income.

According to an article entitled "A Brief History of Congregational Song" (Liturgies, Sonreign Media, Inc.), "Since 1950, there has been more music published for congregational singing than at any other time in the history of the church. Nearly every major denominational body, as well as many independent congregations and publishing companies, have produced official and supplementary hymnals and related collections of songs."

In an interesting blog post called, "Why Men Have Stopped Singing In Church," David Murrow observes that the overwhelming amount of worship songs we feed our congregations may have a negative effect, and that our congregations are over-saturated by way too much. He wryly adds, "In short order we went from 250 songs everyone knows to 250,000+ songs nobody knows."

In response to this dilemma, Murrow states that men "...are doers, and singing was one of the things we used to do together in church. It was a chance to participate. Now, with congregational singing going away, and communion no longer a weekly ordinance, there's only one avenue left for men to participate in the service—the offering. Is this really the message we want to send to men? Sit there, be quiet, and enjoy the show. And don't forget to give us money."

Murrow goes on to suggest that if we are to teach new songs to our congregations, then we must be sensitive and allow time for the songs to permeate into the soul, for the worshiper to become emotionally connected with the material.

"Years ago, worship leaders used to prepare their flocks when introducing a new song. 'We're going to do a new song for you now. We'll go through it twice, and then we invite you to join in'... There's nothing wrong with professionalism and quality in church music. The problem isn't the rock band, or the lights, or the smoke machine. The key here is familiarity. When that super-hip band performed a hymn, the crowd responded. People sang. Even the men."

As the praise and worship phenomenon continues to be a generally positive move forward in congregational singing, we must continually check our motives and methods to assure that Christ is the true focus of our singing, and that our congregations are given the opportunity to make that connection.

Tips for a Successful Rehearsal

Preparation for weekly worship is the foundation for a successful service. We spent a considerable amount of time on the pre-rehearsal phase, now it's time we dive into the actual rehearsal.

Like I said before, I prefer to put a time limit of 90-minutes on rehearsal. In particular situations, such as rehearsal for a special event, it may be necessary to go longer. If we as leaders have our preparations together, we can accomplish much in that hour-and-a-half.

Since we are attempting to have our worship plan prepared two weeks away from service, our teams should be expected to learn new songs on their own, and to make special notes about their parts before rehearsal. It's helpful for the band to look through their charts and highlight repeats, endings and codas, when to rest and when to play a special part. It's helpful if beforehand the singers look over the songs, too, making notes on when to sing in unison or in parts, etc.

Like I stressed in the chapter on pre-rehearsal preparations, it's best for the worship leader to make as many decisions as possible before rehearsal regarding song arrangements, modulations, tempo changes, prayers, stage moves, etc. Thinking through these things, and creating a plan in advance, will help streamline rehearsal. Always make sure that there are plenty of extra charts, lyric sheets, markers and pencils with erasers available for the band and singers during rehearsal.

The important thing to stress about rehearsal is that it *isn't* a time to

Jamie Harvill

learn songs, but instead to **refine** them, and to knit the transitions together for a seamless flow. I've heard it said that *practice* is for private learning and *rehearsal* is for putting it all together with the team. The rehearsal leader must keep an eye on time and move things along. Without direction, minutia will cause things to bog down.

When conducting a rehearsal, use these following guidelines:

- Start and end on time! *Actions* speak louder than *words*. Barbara Coloroso, best-selling author of books on parenting, writes about children and consistency; worship teams need consistency, too. She says "Our children [teams] are counting on us to provide two things: consistency and structure. Children [team members] need parents [leaders] who say what they mean, mean what they say, and do what they say they are going to do." (When team members show a lack of commitment and respect for other's time by arriving late to rehearsal on a regular basis, leaders may be prompted to have a heart-to-heart, private discussion with them)

- Make sure each player and singer can hear themselves properly in the monitors before starting run-throughs

- Confirm the written tempo for each song. The drummer is served well if supplied with a metronome for rehearsal. Sometimes it's helpful to connect the metronome feed into the headphone monitors, along with the rest of the mix, so at least the drummer can hear the click when tempos are set (tempos can be deceiving; they may seem fine in rehearsal, but feel slow in the "heat" of the performance. It's best to trust what is decided in rehearsal)

- Talk about transitions between songs as well as any important dynamic issues in a set. Also, it's best when the singers have a lyric sheet with predetermined directions as to where to sing unison, parts, answers, etc. Decide who in the band will start the next song, or if the band will keep rolling out of one song into the next. Make sure the drummer keeps the tempo on the hi-hat during soft sections of songs so especially the singers can stay on the beat together

Worship Foundry

- Run the set, and then talk about any adjustments. Encourage the band to write corrections on their charts, and singers on their lyric sheet for later reference (It's easy to forget changes between mid-week rehearsal and the weekend)

- A special music selection or a new song is the most vulnerable because they have never been performed. Again, preparation is the key. Each team member should be ready to "rough-in" the song at rehearsal...not learn it. Sometimes it's good to take a few minutes out of the week's set to run through a song slated for a future performance

- If a choir is involved in the weekly rehearsal, each choir member must have access to materials in advance, such as lyric sheets and mp3s. It may be more efficient to rehearse the choir and singers separate from the band in the first 45-minutes, and then come together in the second-half to run the songs for the set. All components of the rehearsal are best accomplished within the scheduled 90-minutes

- Record the rehearsal and post a link online for everyone to reference later, if necessary

- Talk through stage moves, entrances and exits, where to pray, when to speak, hand-offs, etc.

- Make sure everyone has the materials and information they need to take home for review. Discuss any special items such as what to wear for the service, and the next call time

- Pray that God will work in the lives of the team through the rest of the week, and for what He will do in the upcoming service. It may also be a good time to have a brief devotion (still within the 90-minute limit), and to promote "family values," vision, and mission; to help focus the team on the "big picture" of what's in store for the congregation during worship services over the coming weeks

Jamie Harvill

Sometimes churches aren't able to have a mid-week rehearsal, for one reason or another. I prefer a mid-week rehearsal to allow a few days before the weekend service to make adjustments.

It's critical to do a tech run-through with everyone before the weekend service—a dress rehearsal of sorts—to smooth out any changes since the mid-week rehearsal. Use this final opportunity to make a practice-run with the projected lyrics to verify that the songs are laid out like the band arrangements, and take the opportunity to look for misspellings, grammar mistakes, correct punctuation, missing words, etc.

This attention to detail will help maintain flow in the service—for the leader and the congregation. It's helpful to have a TV monitor out in front of the singers, or a projected image on the back wall of the sanctuary, providing song lyrics that match what the congregation is seeing. With the proper system, it also allows the front-of-house mixer or service producer to discretely post important messages. It's also a handy place to put a countdown clock to help keep the pastor and worship leader on track (a necessity for synchronizing services in a multi-site and/or multi-venue church).

When the pre-service run is finished, clear the stage of any trash or loose items like cups, purses, briefcases, etc., and encourage the team not to stand around and talk onstage before the service. It's helpful to have a full 30-minutes of time, if possible, between concluding the pre-service run and the start of the service.

Be ready for surprises and expect spiritual resistance. The enemy would want nothing more than to disrupt the service. Things can, and will, go wrong at times in the service. So, prepare "escape routes" if anything does goes awry. Always be *as ready as possible* to catch something before it has the opportunity to derail a service. Sometimes we can successfully recover a fumble—sometimes we might not be so fortunate. But it's always helpful to have as many *answered questions* as possible before the service begins. With prayer, a plan, patience and practice, God will do mighty things. Just wait and see!

SECTION 5:
THE WORSHIP SERVICE

Engaging the Congregation

When I set out on my music career, the first thing I learned from my mentors at *American Entertainment Productions* was to *connect with the audience*. I was taught that the stage is not a fish bowl, where the audience peers statically at the action happening on stage. The potent energy that flows back and forth from the performer to the audience is a very important aspect of the presentation. That is why live performances haven't been completely obliterated by movies and television; people still desire that back-and-forth, "being there" camaraderie of a live program.

The concept of "entertainment" in the context of worship is a sensitive subject in many church circles. But as I've said before, using musical and dramatic techniques to enhance the art of storytelling and communicating the Gospel can help create a flowing and enjoyable worship experience— one that allows the audience to lose its self-awareness, to the point where they are fully engaged in what's happening on the stage. To make sure that I'm not misunderstood, I want to emphasize that delivering the message of Christ and His redemptive power is, by far, the most noble and virtuous use of the stage, cutting-edge technology, and excellence in all means of effective communication and performance.

Jamie Harvill

Performance Myths

The perspective of the audience is obviously different from that of the performer. Tom Jackson, a professional live performance producer, helps bands develop their live shows to effectively deliver a powerful performance. In a teaching from one of his DVDs entitled *Stage Performance: Making Our Services Rock*, Tom speaks of several myths from a performer's point of view:

- If we *feel* the music then the audience must *feel* it, too
- It's all about the song [that the song itself is strong enough to carry the performance]
- If we play well, sing well, and the audience hears the words, we win
- There are no performance rules—we just "wing it" because we are spontaneous
- "I've been doing it for 'X' amount of years; I know what I'm doing"
- I feel comfortable onstage, so it *must* be great
- If I'm uncomfortable, it must not be "me"
- If it worked for a bigger church then it will work for me

The difference between a great performance and an average or poor performance is essentially the *connection with the audience*. Jackson made a humorous but accurate observation of a great performer, referring to Bono, lead singer of the rock band U2, as an example. He said Bono is "married" to the audience, when most of us are just "dating" the audience. It takes a great amount of skill to bring a great performance, and in doing so, **we earn the audience's respect**. I've personally seen U2 perform live and Bono had everyone in that gigantic indoor sports arena in the palm of his hand!

Three Performance Basics
1. Connect with your audience (Love them and they'll love you back).
2. Lead your audience (They want to follow you!).
3. Your audience is less aware than you may think (Keep your mistakes to yourself).

The **#1** thing to remember in a performance is: **Connect with your audience**, be prepared and confident. Practice to the point where everything you do is from the subconscious—as if the effort was second-hand. That way,

Worship Foundry

your body language will reflect confidence and fluidity rather than being stiff and awkward. A performer's ability to be authentic, warm and engaging—yet humble—helps to build confidence within the audience. When a performer exudes a lack of confidence, the audience feels unsure, expecting him to make a mistake or misspeak. *Preparedness leads to confidence!*

The #2 thing to remember is: **The audience wants to be led**. We help the audience along on our journey through:

- Directing their attention toward important aspects of the performance with *visual and verbal cues* (please stand; please sit; "Let's welcome to the stage X, Y or Z"; "Please direct your attention to the video screens"; musical cut-offs; when to applaud, etc.)
- Giving them permission to respond appropriately
- Helping them move through transitions in the performance without losing focus

Don't take for granted that the audience knows what to do...they don't! Your job as a *leader* is to *lead them*!

The #3 thing to remember is: **The audience is unaware**. I could say ignorant, but that would be a little harsh. The audience is not as aware of the intricacies of our performance as we are. Things aren't always as obvious to the audience until we direct their attention toward something. Many times our mistakes will go unnoticed if we simply move on without acknowledging them. Though this obviously does not apply in relationships, we must remain confident and in control.

I once heard it said, "My play was a complete success but the audience was a failure!" But in reality we cannot blame a poor performance on the audience. A lack of preparation and planning will surely come back to bite us later on the stage. Very few great artists "wing it." A great performance, whether in worship or on a secular stage, is scrutinized for every move, action and spoken word. The key for every performer, worship leader or preacher is to make what they do seem effortless.

"Smile Real Loud!"

I've learned a lot during my time on the road, and performing for more than 40 years. I've learned to make quick decisions when something get

Jamie Harvill

off track. The greatest stage performers make it look easy. Part of the secret is being comfortable with one's self. In fact, talent is only one of several ingredients in a successful stage presentation. You see, *people hear with their eyes*. Tom Jackson says that "communication is 15% words, 30% tone and emotion, and 55% what the audience sees."

Many years ago, the Carter Sisters were performing with their mother, the legendary Maybelle Carter. The audience couldn't hear the bass fiddle in the P.A. system. So in her infinite wisdom, Mother Maybelle leaned toward the daughter who was playing the bass and whispered, "Just smile real loud!" This is good advice for any performer.

One time, after arriving in Houston for a concert, our band equipment hadn't shown up at the venue as expected. The performance was just hours away, but to our horror, when the gear truck did finally arrive, everyone's equipment was accounted for except for the drummer's—only the snare drum showed up. As road manager and leader of the band, I turned to my brother Jon, the drummer, with the bad news. I had no choice but that *the show must go on*. I knew for Jon it would be like doing a waltz on one leg! With trepidation and mild protest, he eventually adjusted to the circumstances (as a consummate professional does) and did the gig—with flair, by the way. Jon learned to "smile real loud," and received compliments on his drumming!

I do everything in my power to avoid these types of situations. But when things happen beyond our control, know that there are options available, maybe not ones we prefer. Just make sure to bring tap shoes in your gig bag!

During another concert, I was just about to play a guitar solo when my amplifier decided to quit. I could have panicked, but my "show must go on" training screamed louder than "go hide under a rock!" So, in a split-second I decided to do the solo anyway, just this time there was no sound. I even made a home-plate slide at the end of it, and came to an abrupt halt just as the audience started to cheer. I not only survived a potential tragedy, but made an even better performance out of the mishap. Several people in the audience came up after the show and complimented me on my great solo! You see, they actually heard nothing...what they saw, though, made them think they heard the solo! (I will address more on the subject of "when things go wrong" in chapter 23, later in this section).

Worship Foundry

Looking Into the Eyes of the Audience

When I play guitar in a band setting, and am not leading or singing, I take the opportunity to look out into the audience and make mental notes about the human landscape. It's kind of like when you travel in the back seat of a car as a passenger without having the responsibility of driving, and you notice things you never could if you were at the wheel. As I scan the audience, even if I am not looking at anyone in particular, individuals in the audience perceive that I'm looking right at them. I love to make connections like that.

Having fun onstage is infectious and the audience will follow suit. I love performing for people, and I especially love it when the audience and performer become one, and everyone forgets that we're in the auditorium—that's when the fun begins!

A Common Emotional and Spiritual Experience

James Taylor, the great singer-songwriter, is a master at engaging his audience. I had the opportunity to see him in concert several years ago, and his "aw-shucks" demeanor during the performance was endearing. He has the gift of disarming his listeners, helping them to relax—to take it all in and forget about their troubles for a while.

James has said that a live performance is a *common emotional experience* for the performer and the audience. As performers, we must plan, prepare and practice for a performance. But there comes a time when we must surrender to the moment—to be fully "present" in our live performances and let things unfold. That's why each performance, even though they contain the same elements, can be received and enjoyed in various ways by different audiences.

When I lead worship, I am aware that each audience and service is unique; the same exact group of people will never assemble again—we will never lead worship the exact same way again either.

This shared emotional experience is the goal of our worship services. Not only are the worship leader, band and singers joining with the audience, but we all join our hearts together with the God of the universe. This makes worship time a *sacred time*. It's not just a concert or performance that we are putting on, but an opportunity to commune together as the Body of

Jamie Harvill

Christ with Almighty God. What we experience in a wonderful time of worship can be life-changing. So, to serve our God and congregations well, we must purpose to raise the performance level of our services as high as possible.

Fish Out of Water

Sometimes as musicians and singers we are a certain way onstage—lifting hands in the air, clapping, dancing and rocking to the music being performed—but we are an awkward mess as audience members, like a fish out of water when the music starts.

It's healthy for a performer to be an audience member from time to time because it helps us see what everything looks like from the congregation's perspective.

Many musicians say that Nashville audiences are the worst on their itinerary, most likely because the crowd is filled with fellow musicians and singers. The tendency for musicians is to stand there, cross-armed and blank-faced, not giving needed feedback to the performers on stage.

In an online article, guitarist and singer Tommy Shaw sheds light on this fish-out-of-water sensitivity—when performers are at their most vulnerable state. Recalling an award show where he and his group, Styx, had recently performed, Shaw said:

> "Having attended enough shows, I have finally come to the conclusion that I am not a lone freak, I am in a class of freaks of artists that just don't know what to do with themselves from that [audience member] perspective. Looking out that night at the audience, brightly lit because the event was televised, I could see them all...So there we were starting into "Blue Collar Man" when I looked out and saw them: Artists, musicians, their spouses and dates, their handlers and relatives everywhere, most of them friends...I recognized that look on their faces—awkward helplessness and 'fish-out-of' water' syndrome...I think artists will agree, we just don't know what to do when we are audience members. It's difficult to suspend your disbelief as an audience member because you have too

Worship Foundry

much experience from the stage and you instinctively take on the same reflex reactions as if you were up there, except now you are helpless because you are not in the mix."

The problem extends to the church where pastors and worship leaders have the same difficulties. There is nothing more frustrating than to see the pastor on the front row, fiddling with his sermon notes during a tender moment in worship, or a worship leader checking email on his smart-phone during a sermon or a time of prayer.

If we expect our audiences to join with us on the worship journey, then when it's time to be an audience member ourselves, we must be willing to participate and give those on stage our full attention.

Assessing Your Performance Habits

Just like Tommy Shaw said, during his performances he scans the audience. One of the most important things a music team can do, while keeping an ear on the performance, is to continually scan the audience and find a section of people to whom you feel comfortable playing. Lifting your eyes off of the music stand and into the audience, away from your keyboard, guitar, drums or bass, is a key way to engage the audience.

It's a good thing to look at videos of your own stage performance and mannerisms. Some people scowl without realizing it. Some look down at their instrument all the time. The key here is to learn to look positive and to keep your eyes up as much as possible, looking into the audience. It's amazing when a group is energized, positive, engaging and warm—all at the same time. From the audience's perspective, this makes the band sound even better!

The important distinction between leading worship and any other performance is that the band and singers are worshiping together with the congregation. It's important that every person on the stage is engaged in worship. Every musician and singer is important to the overall presentation.

Stage Zones

The stage can be divided into three zones. This helps to distinguish the roles of each member in the overall performance. These zones are:

- The Front-line Zone
- The Mid-stage Zone
- The Back-line Zone

Front-Line Zone

The persons in the front-line zone include the *lead singer, worship leader* and many times the *background singers*.

The worship leader has a multi-functional role on stage, including a direct connection to the audience. It's the leader's job to connect emotionally with the audience, to help create continuity between songs and segments, to be sensitive to the Holy Spirit, to give the audience directions to sit, stand, applaud, and guide the audience to focus on certain elements of the service.

The worship leader is the key person on stage for the audience, so it's imperative that the leader is comfortable looking out into the audience throughout the service, scanning and connecting with each section of the auditorium—up, down and from side to side. The other members of the front-line zone may not speak directly to the audience, but they must also look into the audience and engage them during the service with positive and confident body language.

Jamie Harvill

Mid-stage Zone

The persons in the mid-stage zone include the *solo musicians*, other *harmony singers* and *instrumentalists*, and ones that have the *ability to move around onstage*.

As mid-stage performers, these members aren't as responsible for directly connecting with the audience through verbal communication, but when they take a solo, for instance, they must be able to step out from their fixed place on stage to play or sing with confidence. It's also important that persons from the other zones turn and help focus attention on the featured soloist. This, in turn, helps the audience direct its attention to the appropriate place on stage. The team can do this with very subtle movements in order to keep the visual flow going from section to section of each song.

Sometimes a lead guitarist will share the front-line, so it's easier to direct attention to a solo when they are already in a more visible place on stage. **Avoid turning your back to the audience**, which is generally thought of as a rude gesture. Instead, carefully walk backward, if possible, to return to your fixed position on stage.

Back-Line Zone

The back-line zone is where the *bass player, drummer, percussionist, horns, strings*, and sometime *auxiliary keyboards* are placed.

This zone is made up of musicians who are necessarily anchored in their positions on stage, and are not physically mobile like the players in other zones (with the possible exception of a solo horn player who may move into the mid-stage or front-line zones for a solo).

Being two zones back from the front-line doesn't diminish the visual importance of the performance from these musicians. Drummers and percussionists have the potential to bring tremendous visual energy to the stage as they display the most physical movement of all the musicians. When the bass player, percussionist and drummer are locked-in together on a particularly strong rhythmic section of a song, they can easily pull focus away from the front-line.

Horn players can also add to the visual look of a performance. They must also pay close attention to the other musical elements on stage—engaging

Worship Foundry

with the audience and with other members—not just their charts on the music stands in front of them.

It's important that each member of the band and the singers engage each other on stage, which helps lift the visual energy by simply having a great time playing and singing.

It's equally important to show sensitivity when the musical and spiritual moments shift. Matching the appropriate gestures with the musical mood will help support the moment rather than cause a distraction. More somber musical moods will require less physical movement, but each player and singer must be aware that, at this point, even subtle facial expressions will either support or distract from the moment.

Players and singers must always remember that at least one person in the audience is looking at them at any given time during a performance. So it's important to be fully engaged and an active part of each section of the service, even when not playing or singing.

Musician Sight-Lines

It's important, from a staging perspective, that the placement of each musician and singer looks balanced from the audience. But for the sake of musical communication, the band must also be physically arranged so that each individual has a proper sight-line to one another.

The drummer and bass player have a close musical relationship, so arrange them where the bass player is positioned close-in on the hi-hat-side of the drum kit.

The other members of the band need to have a direct sight-line with the musical director as well, for count-ins, cut-offs and tempo changes. A horn section and/or string section must be able to see the director, but it's not as important for them to be in a sight-line with the band.

Arranging for Band and Vocals

The Band

The popular music of today is highly influenced by improvisation. Jazz, bluegrass, blues, country, rock 'n' roll and gospel music genres have all developed out of a free-form style that encourages individual creativity.

Most church music prior to the worship revolution was largely pre-orchestrated, giving little opportunity for musicians to improvise. As mentioned before, the popularity of praise and worship music opened the door to use guitar, bass and electric keyboards in worship services. These days, most worship bands develop arrangements on their own, based on the original artist recordings. As a result of this creative freedom, it's tempting for worship musicians to over-play.

Listening Skills and Musical Discipline

Song arrangements are developed organically for most worship bands. Even with a proper chord chart, it's left to each player to determine their specific parts. Listening skills and musical discipline are learned-traits for most players, and unless we as leaders promote excellence of musicianship within our worship teams, the result will be confusion, and we will continue to dog paddle in musical mediocrity.

The following paragraphs contain very helpful information, beginning

Jamie Harvill

with the all-important **100% Rule**, and concluding with a list of 10 tips to help launch your worship band to the next musical level.

The 100% Rule

It's important to set a goal or standard for each player to maintain dynamics and musicality. This is best illustrated by using the 100% rule.

Using the diagram below, we see that when a single instrument plays a song's accompaniment, the player can make use of 100% of the musical landscape: rhythm, bass, chord movements, etc. But when another instrument joins the accompaniment—such as an acoustic guitar with a piano, for instance—each must adjust their playing to cover 50% of the musical landscape.

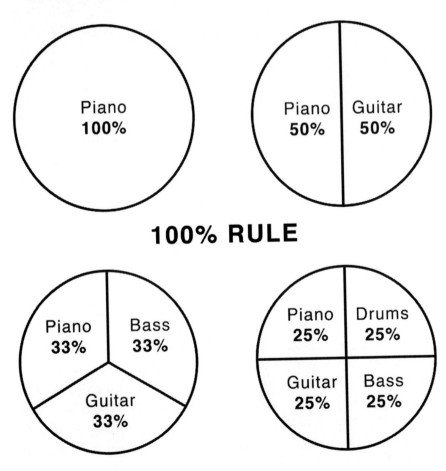

Worship Foundry

When a bass player joins the band, the keyboardist can now focus less on their left hand-playing (bass), and the guitar can now focus on chord placement higher on the neck, away from the range occupied by the keys. Now 33% musical space is given to each of the three instruments.

When a drummer joins the band, the other players can relax even more to make room for the new instrument. It's no longer necessary for the piano, acoustic guitar and bass to carry the bulk of the rhythmic responsibility. Though the rhythm is still somewhat shared, each player must be careful to avoid wandering into the other players' territory. As a result, each person can play even less: 25% each, and so on. *The successive addition of instruments will result in each person having to play less.*

To hear examples of "building block" playing, listen to the complex harmonic and rhythmic construction techniques of groups like *Earth, Wind and Fire* and *Coldplay*. Paying close attention, one can hear that each individual instrumentalist is playing relatively simple parts. But by pulling back and listening to the big picture, interactions between the musical elements create an intricate but satisfying sum total. In other words: *a big sound can be created by interweaving smaller, simpler parts.*

In all of my experience playing live and in the studio, I find that the three "Ls" of good musicianship are: Listen. Listen. Listen. When a musician learns to pay close attention to what the others are doing, and realizes that playing in a band is more about creating a conversation than each person making a speech, the music benefits tremendously.

Sonic Space and the Frequency Spectrum

Each instrument fills a sonic space within the frequency (or tonal) spectrum. Keyboards, vocals and guitars share a similar frequency range, so it's easy for parts to become "blurry" or covered up when everyone plays in the same space. For instance, when a piano part is centered around mid-keyboard (middle-C), and to make each part distinctive, it's helpful for the guitarist to occupy another tonal space in another octave.

Also, when using more than one guitar—and to create a bigger, more diverse sound—each guitarist must decide where on the neck to play: one guitarist high on the neck, and the other in a lower position. Sometimes an electric guitar can make a huge musical statement by playing a simple part on a single string with a creative effect like a delay or tremolo.

145

Jamie Harvill

Two keyboardists can choose between two different sounds and create complimentary parts to play.

It's important to be creative and experimental when choosing unique sounds for each part. This will help to diversify the tonal pallet, making it easier for each part to be heard in the mix. Remember, sound techs constantly battle while mixing a band whose musicians don't carefully select simple, yet well-composed parts. When everything has its place in the mix, music can be a powerful force!

Here are 10 tips on playing economically, musically and skillfully:

1. **Choose economical parts to play.** Using the 100% rule as a guide, learn to play less as other instruments are added to the band. Sometimes go high, sometimes low—whatever is needed to advance the song. Develop a signature "riff" or a distinctive instrumental melody in the *intro, turnarounds* and *outro* of the song. Well constructed parts are the starting-point for a great sounding band.

2. **Make use of dynamics.** Listen to each other. Don't play at all when the music doesn't call for it (what a concept!). Verses can be softer than choruses to create dynamics within a song. A song's power in worship is diminished when everyone plays full-blast, all the time. Like a good novel, think of a song as having a beginning, middle and end; decide which parts and instrumentation will be layered in and out to create an ebb and flow within the song.

3. **Everyone play the same chord progression.** A well organized chord chart is essential for each player, displaying chords with corresponding rhythmic movements.

4. **Pay attention to the finer details.** Solidify each rhythmic highlight, whole-note, dynamic rise and fall, and tempo change. Make sure everyone is accenting at the same place, at the same time.

5. **Check tuning often.** Make sure the band is in tune. Check that the keyboards are in correct concert pitch (A-440)—settings can be mistakenly changed if a keyboard player is not careful. Guitar

Worship Foundry

and bass players need to continually check their tuning (silently, please!).

6. **Make sure everyone can hear and see.** Everyone in the band must be able to hear themselves and each other (in-ear monitors, floor wedges, etc.), and see each other on stage. Utilizing good monitoring and having proper sight-lines between band members is essential for proper musical communication.

7. **Use a click.** A click/metronome (for the drummer alone or in the headphones of the band) is helpful to insure that the predetermined tempo is followed. Tempos that feel right in rehearsal may feel either too slow or too fast during performance—stick to what you decide beforehand. The drummer usually operates the click, so allow for enough time to adjust tempos between songs.

8. **Be generous.** Give musical space for others to fill. Don't be selfish; give opportunity for everyone in the band to shine. The most important thing is to prefer each other in love (Romans 12:10), and for the collective, disciplined efforts of each player to focus on the betterment of the whole.

9. **Play in time.** Don't rush the beat, which is the most common trait of a novice player on the team. Be careful, when necessary, to lay back the beat in a musical fashion. Practice with a click. Make sure everyone hears plenty of hi-hat from the drummer, especially the singers (who may not be able to hear the click).

10. **Pay attention to tone.** Good tone is subjective for each player, but it can be agreed that one's instrument must be warm and full-sounding—without the annoying hiss of white-noise, static, or the rumble of 60-cycle electrical hum. A pleasing tone originates from well crafted instruments and amplifiers (vacuum tubes, speakers and components); high-quality cables; quality effects; proper microphone technique and direct-input devices with good transformers. Don't expect to sound like your favorite rock star simply because you buy the same gear that they use. "Bone Tone"—the individuality that comes from your unique touch—can be a

good thing! Get help from a musician whose tone and playing you admire to guide you toward your own signature sound.

It's helpful to record your band in a live environment whenever possible—it will tell the truth about how you really sound. Your team will benefit from your hard work, and your church will, too. But the most important thing is to become a great worship band for the glory of God! These tips will get you started, but the constant pursuit of excellence will keep you stretching for higher levels of tone and musicianship.

The Vocalists

Peter Yarrow, of the folk group *Peter, Paul and Mary* fame, has said, "When people sing together, community is created. Together we rejoice, we celebrate, we mourn and we comfort each other. Through music, we reach each other's hearts and souls. Music allows us to find a connection." From *Peter, Paul and Mary's* 25th Anniversary Concert DVD, Yarrow made another poignant statement about honesty and singing, and the importance of audience participation: "The sound of your voices is a part of the glue that holds us together, because we know the kind of people that you are from the way that you sing. We know that we could invite you to our homes and you'd help us do the dishes. We also know the kind of hearts you've got [with] the sung word, it's very hard to lie with your voice when you're singing; you really hear what's inside you."

Singing is probably the purest form of music. Many a fine musician has found inspiration in the human voice when playing their instrument. The human voice is directly connected to the soul, and through the voice one can hear pain, joy, tenderness, aggression, as well as a myriad of other articulations that mirror human emotion.

Creating Great Vocal Arrangements

Like I've stated several times already, the congregation in worship is the "lead singer," and since their vocal range is very limited, pick a key where the melody stays within the *Bb below middle-C to D, an octave and a major-second above middle-C* range. (See Congregational Singing Range chart in chapter 19).

Worship Foundry

It may, at times, be necessary for the worship leader to pass on the melody part of certain songs to another person on the team. Even though they may take a harmony part, the worship leader can still guide the congregation through the songs as usual.

When a suitable key is chosen for a song, the vocal team can pick harmony parts to sing. Just like the band, the arrangements usually develop organically, with help from the vocal arrangement on the original recording.

I've been asked several times about how to develop great vocal arrangements. For me, it's all about creating a beginning, middle and an end to a song, which then helps it to blossom all the way to the final note. The tendency for some is to have everyone jump in, find a note, and sing everywhere.

The following are some helpful tips to take your vocal arrangements to the next level. I have included both technical and musical hints to help give your song a place to develop and grow, and to inspire the congregation to join with you on the worship journey.

Of course, it's important to correctly warm-up before vocalizing!

<u>10 Tips for Creating Great Worship Vocals:</u>

1. **Confidence.** This is so important because a vocalist is a high-profile position on the worship team. They are the most visible people on stage, next to the worship leader. An individual's confidence will set the congregation at ease as they help lead the singing. A singer's confidence in their musical abilities and feeling comfortable onstage will help to project positive body language.

2. **Find and stay on your part.** Tenors usually gravitate toward the harmony part right above the melody (following the major-third part of the chord progression); altos usually gravitate toward the harmony part above the tenor (following the fifth-note of the chord progression). Sometimes the melody will require the tenor and alto to "flip" parts, where the alto takes the major-third above the melody, and the tenor takes the fifth (pun intended), this time below the melody. Good harmony singers will be able to "flip" parts when needed. Avoid absolute parallel singing—it leads to

Jamie Harvill

an occasional gospel-sounding 7th and 6th, which may not be desirable for modern rock styles of worship.

3. **Unison, 2- and 3-part harmony**. Start songs with either a solo lead vocal or a unison group vocal to establish the melody for the congregation. Then split-off into either 2- or 3-part harmony in the chorus to create a bigger sound. A single-harmony part (tenor: 3rd above melody) will make the second verse stand up a little more than the first verse, but will leave somewhere for the song to progress into the second chorus. Using this layering technique will help create contrast between sections and will build musical interest. Some modern rock styles require less vocal harmony, so a single line—a 3rd above the melody in each chorus—may be all that's necessary.

4. **Dynamics.** It's the lead singer's job to set the pace for vocal dynamics. If the song requires a breathy vocal sound, the whole vocal group should follow suit, and the same when there's a need for a more aggressive vocal styling. The goal is for the vocal team to sync with the lead vocalist. Sometimes dynamics can be achieved by having less or more people sing; sometimes through the varying of volume.

5. **Blend.** Sing like a group, not as individuals. Eliminate excessive vibrato and other undesirable qualities that cause individual voices to jump out within the mix. A vocal section leader—which may be the worship leader or a music director— must take responsibility for mapping out the song for phrasing and blend. It's so important for each vocalist to hear their part and the other singers, therefore, a proper monitor mix is essential. When singers don't hear themselves, they tend to over-sing. Great blend starts with singing on pitch!

6. **Phrasing.** Good phrasing is singing a musical line so that it sounds effortless, not rushed; easy and carefree. When a song's melody and lyric is complex, it's a good practice to map out which notes to hold, and which to cut short. It's important to find appropriate places to breathe, where to pause and where to scoop or taper note

Worship Foundry

endings. Good phrasing helps to tell the story of the song, and it emphasizes the emotion—if it's soft and delicate or energetic and aggressive. When vocalists sing together, they must sing as if they are "one voice," paying close attention to ending consonants like **Ps**, **Ts**, and **Ss**.

7. **Proper microphone technique.** Out of insecurity, an inexperienced singer on the worship team will tend to hold the microphone away from their mouth. It's important that they hold the mic at chin-level, and at an angle suitable for capturing the voice, but not directly in front of the mouth (the area between the chin and the bottom lip is a good place to start). It's important for the audience to see the singer's facial expressions and articulation of the lyrics. Most microphones used in live-music settings are *dynamic mics* (utilizing a moving coil—kind of like a speaker in reverse—to deliver quality, consistency and durability, with a high resistance to feedback). Therefore, since a dynamic mic is best positioned close to the sound source, encourage the vocalists to keep the mic as close to their mouth as possible whenever they sing. The sound mixer will love you for it!

8. **Matching chords.** Be sure that the vocalists are aware of the chord changes in a song to ensure correct harmonization. Pay attention to embellished chords like minor-7ths, major-7ths and major-9ths, and be sure to add the correct notes to create those chords. Pay attention to chords like suspended-2nds and 4ths, and make sure that the vocal team is singing the suspended notes and resolving with the band. Nailing down these details will make or break a vocal sound, and will ensure definition in the final band/vocal mix.

9. **Let the congregation take a solo.** Build a time in the worship set for the congregation to sing all by themselves. It may be helpful for the worship leader to sing along softly, and for the band to lower their volume, but the congregation will appreciate it. They may seem reluctant the first few times, but soon they'll learn to jump in and sing with passion.

Jamie Harvill

10. **To fill or not to fill.** So many of our favorite worship songs were originally recorded in live settings, where it's characteristic for the worship leader, or an assortment of soloists, to add "fills" (using certain words from the lyric for dynamic and emotional impact, or non-word vocalizations such as "ooh" or "aah") between phrases. This helps create excitement and helps "feed" the congregation subsequent lyrics. When it's overdone, though, doing fills or vocal licks can get annoying. It's best to figure out where and who will do licks beforehand in rehearsal to avoid confusion. Less is more, so make sure that a fill, or any kind of talking between songs is necessary. If a set-up isn't needed, then let the song speak for itself!

The Choir in Modern Worship

The choir has taken a back seat in many churches over the past few decades. The worship band and a smaller group of vocalists have supplanted the once ubiquitous worship triumvirate: the piano, organ and choir.

Since choirs in many churches have diminished, print music companies have felt the sting of a shrinking market. Many churches that have maintained a choir are using print music for seasonal performances, musicals and anthems, but seem to have taken a more pedestrian approach when it comes to developing arrangements for songs within the worship set. Many choir directors create simple two- to three-part arrangements to accompany the pop-musical stylings of modern worship.

Youth choirs have diminished over the years as well, and for similar reasons as the adult choir. The result is that children and youth are slowly losing the opportunity to practice the skill of reading music and the discipline of singing pre-arranged vocal parts. This unfortunate trend is finding its way into public school systems throughout North America as budgets are being slashed, subsequently wounding (or killing) vulnerable performing arts programs.

Without a choir program—beginning with children, and graduating into youth and then to adults—the church will lose an important aspect of music education that has distinguished it for decades, even centuries. Since a large percentage of public schools are opting out of music as a course of study—and the church has, for the most part, chosen to cut back

Worship Foundry

or abandon the choir—at some point we will become a musically illiterate culture. Here are some disturbing realities we are facing today:

- Children are losing the opportunity to learn about vocal music, how to sing parts, read musical notation, and experience the discipline, cooperation, and pure joy of singing in a choir
- The use of superb sacred choir literature will continue to decline, denying future generations the honor and pleasure of hearing and singing glorious choral arrangements from some of history's greatest composers and arrangers
- Church music programs will eventually be filled with illiterate musicians, which will limit the songs they will be able to use in worship, and restrict the scope of musical styles that they'll be able to cover

As a response to this frightening scenario, I pray that modern worship leaders take the initiative to bring back the choir, and instrumental music programs, for that matter.

The More Voices the Merrier

A choir in worship will certainly heighten the energy of a service. Techniques mentioned in the "10 Tips for Creating Great Worship Vocals" is a great place to start when building custom arrangements for your church.

Choir should not be the "dumping ground" for the worship ministry. It's important to audition prospective choir members to make sure they can sing on pitch and to find their vocal range. A single vocalist with a bad voice can be heard above all the rest, so it's important to be somewhat selective. There is a bit of grace involved here, as a choir is built on vocal *sections*, historically distinguished by bass, tenor, alto and soprano ranges. The weight of each section is carried by several singers, so naturally, the better vocalists will become leaders in the section and will help those with lesser abilities to remain on part and hopefully in tune. The choir is a great place for those who desire to participate musically in worship, but do not have the vocal ability to join the vocal team. Therefore, the musical requirements may be different for the choir and the vocal team.

Jamie Harvill

Choir Rehearsal

It's helpful to rehearse the choir separately from the worship team. It may be necessary for another person to direct the choir, so that the worship leader can rehearse the band and vocals separately until all three can come together for a joint rehearsal.

Some choirs are slated to perform with the worship team each week. Others are scheduled to perform a few times per month. In any event, it's helpful to develop what my friend, Jason Sears, calls a "frenetic, fast-paced learning environment," where the choir is taught to quickly learn their part. Jason says the process is intense, that he pounds out the parts on his keyboard until the kinks are ironed out and the dynamics are all there. He holds the choir rehearsal to one hour each week.

My friend, Steven V. Taylor—with whom I served alongside as worship leader for almost a decade—created a communicational shorthand with his choir. He trains them to find their parts quickly, and they follow him instinctively; they've learned his patterns and his on-the-fly method of arranging so well, they can quickly pull together an amazing sound—the choir actually becomes Steve's instrument!

Quick Choir Arrangements

A simple rule-of-thumb for quick choir arrangements in the context of a worship set is to either sing the first verse in unison with the melody, or let the leader sing alone. Then have the choir split into either two- or three-part harmony on the choruses. The subsequent verses can grow, with two-part harmony, if desired. The secret weapon with the choir is its ability to use dynamics for great effect. For instance, when a song breaks out into a vocal/drums-only section, the choir can really add power and punch by singing with passion, using high volume and bold intensity. The converse is true on softer passages, when the choir sings softly under the lead singer to create a heavenly, angelic effect. Again, refer to the "10 Tips for Creating Great Worship Vocals" section for more ideas to enhance your "on-the-fly" choir arrangements

When learning an anthem, or preparing a seasonal program, it's best to give the choir a recording of the arrangement, along with the printed music several weeks in advance. Just like the worship team, learning a song can be done individually, on the choir member's own time. The song can be kneaded, chiseled and perfected in choir rehearsal over the ensuing weeks. A disciplined director will offer a suitable amount of time for rehearsal before the choir performs a selection. A week or so before the service, the band can then join the choir in rehearsal.

In A Nutshell

Choirs, when trained to be worshipful, can bring a majestic, ethereal quality to our services. A choir and instrumental program will help children, youth and adults learn and practice sight-reading skills on a regular basis. When we incorporate a healthy mix of traditional and modern music in our services, we benefit from a broad range of musical literature, and the church can take its rightful place at the forefront of the arts.

Some churches may choose to remain choir-less, some may choose to incorporate the choir purely into a modern worship setting. Whatever the choice, let's be the best at it, and bring honor to the Lord.

Instrumental Soloists

When incorporating a solo instrumentalist into worship, variety is the key. When a sax player, for instance, plays all of the time, and fills every musical space with a musical lick, it can get old, fast. Encourage the soloist to work with the other players to plan for alternate places to play fills. When not playing, the sax player can pick up a percussion instrument, change to flute, play guitar or keyboard, or even sing harmony. Too much of the same thing can be overwhelming, especially when there is no pre-arranged part to play.

When adding a horn section or a string section, provide a proper arrangement. If the section is not included in a song's arrangement, have them exit the stage, or stand-by while remaining engaged in the service and focused on what's happening on stage. When adding a single cello part to a worship service, provide either a proper arrangement, or give the player a lead sheet beforehand, with a roadmap of the song to follow. Again, when the players aren't needed, have them exit the stage, or remain engaged until they are to play again.

THE WORSHIP SERVICE PRODUCER

In today's modern performance world, it's difficult to expect a worship leader to be everywhere all of the time when it comes to worship services. In the days of old (15-20 years ago!), it was possible for a worship leader alone to manage their job on stage, the folks out at the sound mixer, and everywhere in between. The job of worship leader today is becoming more complex as the technical requirements for our services grow. So it's possible that some churches may need to bring in a service coordinator as a go-between to help fill the gap between the worlds of stage and tech.

This person, who we'll call "the producer," can be a big help to the worship leader during planning, rehearsal and in performance. Their job is to be *objective* musically, and to be familiar with the technology used in the service. Here are a few thoughts about the job of the producer:

> **The producer** is a person who is experienced in areas of performance, technology and music, who will help the worship leader optimize the service's effectiveness by taking the point-of-view of the audience. They must also have a spiritual sensitivity in order to bring helpful, objective critique regarding the spiritual aspects of the service to the worship leader and pastor.

Jamie Harvill

The producer is one who pays close attention to musical arrangements, staging and technical cues and the overall "feel" of the service—especially during rehearsal and the final run-through—to make sure each element is working; they make suggestions on how to improve areas that aren't measuring up to the pre-determined goals of the service.

The producer is the person who goes over the plan just before the service with the tech and worship teams, as well as any others who will take part in the service, including special guests, staff members and the pastor. It's important to have a printed service plan available to each person involved so every stage movement, music cue and tech cue can be discussed and confirmed.

The producer is a person who has the respect of the worship leader, the pastor and the tech leader, and one who isn't afraid to approach the leaders with critique, but sensitive enough to maintain a positive, creative environment. The pastor will need to understand that the producer may have to be very direct at times, not with disrespect, but in a way that will help to promote and maintain excellence.

The producer can be a person in a paid staff position, but possibly a volunteer. It is optimal for the producer to be involved with the worship production team during the planning of each service. But a volunteer producer can take the plan each week, collaborate with the worship leader, and tweak the service during rehearsal, if necessary. There may be a need to make changes between services.

Maybe there's as associate on staff that has another job description during the week, but who is available and can fulfill the job during weekend services. In any event, it will take a person with an extremely broad range of experience to fulfill the requirements of this position.

When a Service Seems Too Slick

At what point is a church service too slick? That's a question I've been pondering lately. Most of the time too slick means that the service doesn't feel authentic—when the preaching or the performers on the team seem to be over-doing it.

When I see a church service that's "over-the-top," I've come to these four general conclusions:

1. **The message is overshadowed by the method.**
   The principle message we must convey during our services each week is the Gospel of Jesus, found in 1 Corinthians 15:3-4, "For what I received I passed on to you as of first importance: that Christ died for our sins according to the Scriptures, that he was buried, that he was raised on the third day according to the Scriptures..." In an earlier passage from 1 Corinthians 5, Paul speaks of our new life in Christ: "Therefore, if anyone is in Christ, the new creation has come: The old has gone, the new is here! (vs. 17)"

   When too much attention is put on the performance—to the point where our cool arrangements, staging, band and singers are a higher priority than the message of Christ—we're heading away from our true purpose. If

Jamie Harvill

our congregation walks away each week talking about the *method* and not the *message*, our services are too slick.

2. **In the desire to create a quality product, the performance seems "over-produced."**
    It's a good thing to have high standards. We must give our best to God by using production and performance skills to help deliver the Gospel. But through our desire to excel, we may lose touch with our audience. Sometimes we try too hard to deliver a simple but profound message, one that can be complicated by gadgets, glitz, disco balls and fireworks. Sometimes our overuse of technology diminishes the human connection with our congregation. Our technology, regardless of its "coolness," must *serve* the message.

3. **The stage setting, lighting and backdrop don't match the emotion of the performance.**
    Our audience will disengage if they sense a disconnect between the emotion of a performance and the feel of the stage. If the song we are using in worship is down-to-earth—with an acoustic feel, conveying an intimate mood—the performance is best supported by a warm, inviting and intimate stage setting.
    A proper stage setting is much like the music in a movie: the feel of the soundtrack will give emotional clues to the audience. If a Jaws-like cue warns of a circling shark, the audience is given a clue that there's imminent danger awaiting the actor. If there's a happy-sounding music cue, then we as an audience have no worries for the actor at all.
    When we design our staging and plan lighting cues, it's important to match the emotion of what's happening onstage at any given time: high-energy lighting for high-energy points of the service—intimate and warm when the mood is more somber. Again, it's tempting to overuse technology. When the emotions of the stage and the song or sermon match, it helps connect the audience with the message.

Worship Foundry

4. **The performer, while trying to connect with the audience, tries too hard and "oversells" through exaggerated facial movements and hand gestures.**

When I started performing professionally in a secular setting, we were taught to "sell ourselves" to the audience. In church, we must still do all we can from the stage to engage our congregations. But because many churches are using video screens, we can now be more subtle with our facial expressions and gestures. We don't have to oversell our performances (like what frequently happens in amateur Broadway-type stage productions) to connect with the audience. It's much more important to be authentic—real and approachable.

When a performer, preacher or musician tries to "oversell," it seems insincere, and this corrupts the delivery and the service will seem too slick—too impersonal.

People want what's real; they want to relate to whoever is on stage at any given time. When a performer is comfortable, they can loosen up, slow down and deliver an authentic, from-the-heart performance.

Even though it might seem unprepared and impromptu, some artists have a technique for disarming the audience, helping them relax. I once toured with an artist who every night, just after he was introduced, would purposely tap the microphone and say, "Is this thing on?" He would then check his piano by hitting a few keys, adjust his chair, and chat with the audience before the first song was even played. As a result, people felt he was talking right to them, one-on-one—almost like he was in their living room. In return, the audience gave him their complete trust, devotion and full attention. He was a master at owning the space, disarming the audience— coaxing them into the palm of his hand!

Our challenge in planning our services, and to avoid being too slick is: *To be authentic in our delivery, submissive to the direction of the Holy Spirit, and to invite the congregation on a worship journey where we worship God and share the Gospel in word and in song, so that the*

Jamie Harvill

> *wonder of Jesus follows them from the sanctuary, to their car and into their daily lives.*

Excellence vs. Perfection

Sometimes we give up trying to become better musicians, business people, pastors, parents, etc., because we feel if we can't do it *big* we won't do it at all. And unfortunately, some have equated excellence with perfection. I want to dispel this notion by breaking the two words down into bite-sized pieces. In defining each concept, I hope to help others avoid the destructive sink hole of perfectionism that I've fallen into from time to time. We can find success, peace and satisfaction in life even though we're imperfect people in an imperfect world.

Excellence

I don't see excellence as a destination but rather a road trip—heading out on a God-journey toward bigger and better things that He has planned for us. We need to remember that "...we are God's handiwork, created in Christ Jesus to do good works, which God prepared in advance for us to do. (Ephesians 2:10, NIV)"

My granddaughter, Charlotte, will soon turn one year old. The pediatricians say that she's right on target in overall health, development and size. She tried to crawl up our stairs last week, and if it weren't for us hovering over her like helicopters, we would have spent the rest of the day with her in the emergency room. You see as a baby, Charlotte is doing extremely well; I would consider her an excellent baby. If one were to measure her behavior and physical abilities compared to an adult, though, we would be worried. Thankfully, Charlotte is living up to her baby-sized potential.

Excellence is in play when a person or an organization is operating at their highest potential. They may not have all of the resources, or the strength of the next guy, company or church, but they are maximizing their capabilities and giving it everything they've got. The good thing about excellence is that it has nothing to do with the "next guy." It isn't a comparison game. Again, pursuing excellence is not a destination—it's a state of mind that helps us focus on the best possibilities for our personal

Worship Foundry

lives, our families, our businesses and churches. While on this journey we can still make mistakes, learn from them, and get back on track.

Perfection

Perfection is an unreachable destination. *The Merriam-Webster Dictionary* defines perfection as: being flawless; free from fault or defect. Unfortunately, we humans have already lost the race when it comes to perfection. The Bible defines sin as transgression (violation; crime) against the law of God. In archer's terms, sin is a result of failing to hit the mark of perfection—we've missed the bull's-eye! But glory to God, Scripture says: "For just as through the disobedience of the one man [Adam] the many were made sinners, so also through the obedience of the one man [Jesus] the many will be made righteous. (Romans 5:17, NIV)"

God canceled our sin-debt by the blood of Jesus. Through faith in Christ we no longer have to worry about being perfect: Jesus, the Spotless Lamb, became a perfect sacrifice on our behalf! Perfectionism will always frustrate and disappoint because we will never live up to its demands. When we try to attain perfection in business, as artists, in church, in relationships, etc., we will never be truly content. There will never be perfect symmetry on earth, perfect people, or perfect organizations—and certainly not perfect churches. We need to deal with that fact and get on with life.

Excellence vs. perfection? I choose to travel on the road of excellence. I may hit a bump or two along the way, but I know that if I fix my aim on pleasing God, and offer my very best in every circumstance, I'll hit the bull's-eye every time.

WHEN THINGS GO WRONG DURING A SERVICE

With any performance, things have the potential to go wrong: microphones can stop working; the power can fail, causing silence and darkness; music cues can be missed, etc. Whether it's human error or just some freak accident, problems will arise—and they take us by surprise every time!

In any event, our greatest ally is preparation. A thousand mistakes, and an equal amount of equipment failure, can potentially be avoided by thinking through every possible technical, musical or transitional weakness that may be lurking in our weekly worship plan. Paranoia shouldn't rule our planning process, though. If we plan far enough out from the service, with plenty of time to process the program design, while utilizing the talent and wisdom of our planning team, we can anticipate problems and make corrections.

As I have written before, "flow" is necessary when we are taking our congregations on a weekly journey, maintaining their full and active attention while communicating the message of the Gospel. When things go wrong, their attention is deflected away from the intended focus and toward the distraction. This destroys that precious state of mind which every skilled communicator works for: *the place where the audience is no longer self-aware, time flies and they are fully engaged in the moment.*

Bad things can happen **from the stage** and bad things can happen **from the audience**.

Jamie Harvill

<u>Here are 10 crucial things to keep in mind that may help avoid the most serious of problems:</u>

From The Stage

- Don't do anything from the stage that hasn't been scrutinized and agreed upon collectively by the worship production team. Of course, there will be times when God wants to go in another direction and the pastor or leader of the service will have to make that call. Spontaneity doesn't equal spirituality, though.

- Make sure that the technical aspects of the service are tested and run in rehearsal; go over entrances and exits, and how staging will be moved—who will do what and where, etc., beforehand.

- Make sure that sight lines are established between the leader, band and vocalists. If this isn't possible due to a complicated stage setup, then create an audible means of communication to be used during the service (use wireless, in-ear monitors so that, if needed, the tech team can discretely communicate with the worship leader). To avoid disrupting flow, set pre-determined hand signals or gestures as a means of visual communication between the stage and the people at the sound console.

- When a mistake is made, try not to draw attention to it. Skilled performers know that if they land gracefully on their feet, it is unlikely that the audience will ever be aware of the mess-up.

- If possible, designate a person from the tech team to help with potential staging needs or problems. When called upon, they can inconspicuously move to the stage to take away a prop, fix a sound problem or make an equipment change. It's important that those on stage remain focused. If a problem brings a performance to a screeching halt, it needs to be established beforehand, who will stand in the gap and carry the program until a solution is found, or *to* conclude the service altogether. As said in an earlier chapter: an audience's trust in a good leader will go a long way in helping to get through a distracting moment during a service.

Worship Foundry

From the Audience

- Some churches, pastors and leaders encourage children to sit with their parents during a service. But when disruptions come from babies and small children in the audience, it makes it difficult for others in the service to stay focused on the message. Please don't misunderstand what I'm saying here: I am personally not against having babies or small children in a service. But some churches have policies that limit certain ages from participating in services.

- This is a great opportunity to promote your well-equipped, secure, clean and nurturing childcare facility, and hopefully parents will take their children there before the next service. Not every parent with a screaming baby is going to get up and take them out. It is a delicate situation when a caretaker has to be asked by a worship host to exit with the screaming child.

- Another great way to help with this is by supplying a private and discreet "family room" for parents or caretakers, supplied with a video feed of the service. A separate, private location for nursing mothers will also be very helpful.

- Make it a policy for those who choose to sit toward the front of the sanctuary to remain seated for the entire sermon. Encourage those with physical issues that may require immediate attention to sit where they can exit without disturbing those around them. Sanctuary etiquette must be taught from the pulpit, as well as in membership classes. Pastors and/or worship leaders will have to make a special effort to teach worshipers proper behavior in *casual worship environments.* This may need to be done often, especially in a growing church.

- Train ushers and greeters (worship hosts), in advance of any given service, to be aware of potential interruptions in the audience, and teach them to assist the pastor in a proper and discreet manor when called upon.

Jamie Harvill

- Make sure that a person of authority, other than the one leading from the stage, is available to help contain any situation that may arise during a service. If the pastor or leader makes a gesture from the stage, that appointed person must move quickly toward the disruption or spiritual need in the audience.

- Sometimes a medical emergency may arise during a service. If the ill person is mobile, it's best to handle the situation and attend to their needs with as much discretion as possible until they are stabilized, or until emergency personnel can properly transport them out of the building. Sometimes the person cannot be moved immediately, or without professional medical assistance. But if it's possible, respectfully allow the service to carry on. Plan *in advance* how to approach a medical emergency, and create a predetermined path where emergency personnel can enter and exit the facility with as little disruption as possible.

We can't prevent every disruption from raising its head during our services. Problems will be better managed, though, if we plan for an "escape route" in order to avoid ultimate disaster. Let's face it, to err is human, but to walk right into a problem because of poor planning or laziness is inexcusable!

Garments of Praise (Worship Attire)

Each person on the worship team is considered a leader, and church leaders should exemplify Christian character in conduct, appearance and speech. The fruit of the Spirit passage found in Galatians 5:22-23 is a great place to start when describing appropriate behavior for Christ-followers. According to *The Free Dictionary*, modesty is "regard for decency of behavior, speech, dress, etc." and modest clothing is "...designed to prevent inadvertent exposure of parts of the body."

Godly behavior doesn't draw attention to self, but exalts the Lord. Therefore, it's important that both *men* a*nd women* who take the stage during worship services make wise choices about how they present themselves through their behavior and dress.

Style can be so subjective. Everyone desires to be stylish to some extent, but it must be made clear that any clothing worn on stage that promotes sensuality must be corrected before taking the stage.

A proper dress code must be determined for each church. For instance, I was once a worship leader at a church that required all of the men to wear a jacket and slacks during Saturday and Sunday evening services, and a suit and tie for Sunday morning services. There were no jeans ever allowed on stage during the weekend services. Women were required to wear knee-length dresses at all services. The church I currently serve allows me to wear jeans and a t-shirt during worship, ladies are allowed to wear slacks—quite

Jamie Harvill

a contrast in dress requirements. Interestingly, the style of music for both churches is similar: modern worship.

A Modest Interpretation

Due to the wide interpretation of what proper modest apparel actually is, there must be someone appointed whose duty it is, from week to week, to uphold the dress requirement, and to discretely help the person in question make a change before the worship service begins (a guy for the guys, and a lady for the ladies). If proper training is given to each new member of the worship team in an orientation meeting before their fist time to serve—where a clear list of *dos* and *don'ts* for appropriate dress are given—then for the most part, these uncomfortable pre-service discussions and outfit changes will be unnecessary. If a person continually makes questionable choices about their outfits for worship, it may be a cue to let them take a break until they fully understand the dress code and comply.

Again, those who are on the worship team are leaders, and a place on the stage is not so people can see how cool we look, play or sing. It's rather an opportunity to *serve* the Body of Christ, and to be as transparent as possible while leading worship, in order to draw the congregation's attention *to the Lord*.

Make sure that guest musicians, speakers and singers know your church's dress code in advance, too.

Over the past few decades, church apparel has become much more casual. Gone is the 1950s picture of a church-going family with a suit and tie for the gentlemen, and a dress, hat and gloves for the ladies. Churches with casual environments must work very hard to uphold a standard of modesty with regard to clothing choices. Some folks—guys and gals alike—seem to make downright sensual statements with what they wear to church. I'm not saying we should bar the church doors to forbid people from entering because they don't match the dress requirements posted at the entrance. But we must teach our congregations to make wise choices in what to wear for worship—so as to not create an opportunity for others to stumble in their walk with the Lord. Growing churches may have to address this often, especially in anticipation of the summer months.

Worship Foundry

A Little Help from My Friend

My good buddy—worship leader, singer and teacher, Leann Albrecht—wrote a very helpful blog about proper stage dress for worship. She says: "So, girls...let's be kind to the guys. Don't make it difficult for them. Think of them as a best friend who needs your help to keep a clean thought life. When they look at us, let their first thought be of Jesus..."

She goes on to say: "The same is true for the guys. Tight clothing is not only uncomfortable but distracting. Be kind to the ladies...We, as Christians, need to set a higher standard. A standard that is moral, one that promotes the attitude of Jesus and a lifestyle of purity; one that delights our soul instead of our 'fleshly' senses."

<u>Here are a few more helpful fashion guidelines from Leann:</u>

- "Necklines should not expose cleavage."
- "No tight-fitting clothes for ladies [or gentlemen]; no see-through fabrics. Keep in mind that thin, 'clingy' fabrics are less 'forgiving' than heavier ones. If you're on the stage, remember physical shape is accentuated with bright lighting."
- "Also, for the platform—skirts should be to the knee. Remember, most stages are elevated, which makes the length of a skirt appear shorter from the audience level. If you are sitting on the platform, make sure when you are seated that the skirt is designed to give adequate coverage."
- "No exposed midriffs."

• • •

"Create in me a clean heart, O God, and renew a right spirit within me."
Psalm 51:10 (ESV)

"Blessed are the pure in heart, for they shall see God."
Matthew 5:8 (ESV)

Jamie Harvill

"And it is my prayer that your love may abound more and more, with knowledge and all discernment, so that you may approve what is excellent, and so be pure and blameless for the day of Christ, filled with the fruit of righteousness that comes through Jesus Christ, to the glory and praise of God."
Philippians 1:9-11 (ESV)

"Who shall ascend the hill of the LORD?
And who shall stand in his holy place?
He who has clean hands and a pure heart,
who does not lift up his soul to what is false
and does not swear deceitfully.
He will receive blessing from the LORD
and righteousness from the God of his salvation."
Psalm 24:3-5 (ESV)

SECTION 6:
LEGACY

In an NBC interview with Chris Witherspoon, Oprah Winfrey spoke of leaving a legacy, and recalled an earlier conversation she had about legacy with her mentor, Maya Angelou. Oprah said: "I think the work you have done speaks for you. I remember when I opened my school in South Africa. I said, 'This will be my legacy. This school is going to be my legacy.' And Maya said, 'You have no idea what your legacy will be! Your legacy is what you do every day; it's every life you've touched; it's every person whose life was either moved or not; it's every person you harmed or helped. That's your legacy!' So I don't think about it. I just try to live it."

We may not be able to pick our legacy, but we can choose to live each day with the desire to serve others—to love, to forgive, and encourage as we follow Christ. We can live to glorify God and, in the process, hope to leave a positive impact on the world around us.

Since becoming a Christian decades ago, I have sensed God's call to help others. Nothing energizes me more than helping young people connect with their life purpose and see them flourish in their relationship with the Lord.

Because I'm a teacher at heart, I find myself drawn to people who are

Jamie Harvill

talented, yet humble—willing to learn, and hungry to grow as Christians and musicians. After living for many years near Nashville, Tennessee, I've witnessed people migrating here to pursue their dream of making it big in the music industry. But I tend to stay away from folks whose ambition is to simply "make it big" or to "become a star," because I've seen so many self-centered dreams crash to the ground and break into a million pieces. Fame-seekers, after falling on hard times, eventually wander back to where they came from. Rather, I'm drawn to the talented person with a desire to become the best Christ-follower, musician and leader they can be, and are willing to endure disappointment to follow God's plan for their lives.

I was taught early on to leave a positive legacy—to train others and to help perpetuate the skills I've learned through teaching new generations of ministers, musicians, artists and leaders.

The Apprentice

This type of mentorship reminds me of the merchant and craft guilds during the Middle Ages. Back then, artisans were trained for up to a decade, starting as an apprentice and working without pay under a master craftsman. They would then advance to the paid-position of journeyman, continuing their work under the master. At some point, when they were proven to be experts in their craft, they would be declared master craftsmen themselves. As a result, they could then open up their own shop and train apprentices, and the process started over. *This system of training helped pass down skills, discipline, excellence and quality craftsmanship to new generations, and effectively helped maintain a standard of quality for goods and services.*

College and seminary worship programs are necessary, but we must begin to train future ministers and musicians as early in life as possible. Why can't we have training centers in the local church for young people and new converts, where they can be tutored by "master craftsmen," then released into the world as top-notch ministers and musicians—even before going to college, graduate school or seminary? I believe the church has attempted this to a small extent, but frankly, I think we're intimidated by the size of the task.

Worship Foundry

<u>Here are three general ways to train potential worship musicians and ministers in the church:</u>

- Through a **one-on-one** mentoring relationship with hand-picked students
- Through a mentoring relationship with a **group** of hand-picked students
- Through a general **classroom** format, open to anyone

Mentoring

I thank God for the mentors that came into my life and helped train me for the ministry. I've been guided, molded and counseled by some of the greatest musicians, leaders, songwriters and ministers in the world.

I'm grateful for people like Mary Lewis who, back in '75-'76, reached out and invited me to play guitar for the youth choir when I was a brand-new believer (and very rough around the edges). I am grateful for Wes Turner and Stan Morse from *American Entertainment Productions*. Stan, in particular, believed in me and told me during rehearsal one day: "You're good; you're gonna make it in music one day, just keep going!" As a fledgling minister of music in a small Mobile, Alabama, church, Nancy Gordon (the piano player) unselfishly invited me to write with her after I noticed from the sheet music that she wrote the song we were rehearsing. Her invitation helped open doors to the folks at *Integrity Music*, where I would one day become an exclusive song writer. I thank God for Claire Cloninger and Gerrit Gustafson, who both sat with me and critiqued my songs. (Gerrit even wrote a check to help me purchase the 4-track cassette recorder on which the demo for "Ancient of Days" was recorded.) None of these encounters were earth-shaking, and certainly weren't formal Karate Kid-types of relationships. But they were encounters with very talented people who were willing to slow down and reach out a hand to a struggling artist.

I want to bring the same blessing and encouragement to others who cross my path, and spend time helping them meet their goals and aspirations.

When we recognize persons of exceptional ability and potential, we might be the very person God wants to use in their formative process. Be wise, though, in choosing a candidate, because in one-on-one

Jamie Harvill

discipleship—whether it's spiritual in nature or technical—it's best suited between persons of the same gender. When mentoring persons of the opposite gender, where meetings go on for extended periods of time in private, things can escalate and lead to inappropriate behavior. This cannot be over stated. There may not be a temptation to cross a professional line, but it's important *to never project the appearance of impropriety,* or create a situation where others might misinterpret the relationship. Therefore, it's best for guys to mentor guys, and girls to mentor girls.

Pray about a candidate first, then invite them to talk about their future—what they want to accomplish through their gifts and abilities. Then, if they are willing, help create a plan of action with goals, directives and times of evaluation. Give the disciple an opportunity to "shadow" either you or a person on your team—so they can get hands-on experience in their field. This student/teacher mentoring process can last as long as you both determine.

Group of Hand-Picked Students

This process can be a very effective and efficient use of your time as a teacher. The training is much like the one-on-one process of discipleship just mentioned—with goal setting, evaluation, and hands-on training. These students can be gleaned from those who rise to the top of a general classroom format of training.

I would like to share with you the structure of a student ministry-based music and worship program I started several years ago—and what I named it just so happened to inspire the title of this book.

Worship Foundry

As a teacher, songwriter and musician, I spent a significant amount time in the '90s teaching in worship conferences held all over North America, and throughout the world. During that time, many churches in Asia, and other continents, were making great strides in adopting a modern worship approach to their music programs. Companies like *Integrity Music* and *Maranatha! Music* rose to meet the need and sent teachers like myself all over the globe as "musician-aries." Language barriers didn't stop us as we were given translators for all of our classes.

Worship Foundry

I remember thinking that this type of training didn't need to be limited to a one-and-done regional conference that happened every year or so in someone else's church, city and state. This could be accomplished on a week-to-week basis in one's own home church. In other words, I asked myself: "Why can't we have our own school of worship here in the town where we live?" (This was before the movie "School of Rock" came out.) A big barrier to this idea for a local music school was *organization*. I felt it was important to administer the program to suit the church I was serving, for it to be self-supporting, and to bring on teachers who were considered "masters" at their craft. A tall order indeed!

So many people are intimidated by ideas like this; I certainly was at first. But, as it is said, "A journey of a thousand miles starts with a single step!" I talked with the student pastor over the next several months and we decided to start what was to be called *Worship Foundry*. In the course of two semesters, we enrolled dozens of students. Many of the kids that were in the program have since made the leap into full-time ministry, and are still playing, singing and leading in churches all over the nation. I later served a church where I implemented this program again, and it was even more fruitful and successful than the previous one.

Here's a breakdown of the Worship Foundry program:

1. Class offerings were chosen (guitar 1 & 2, bass guitar, keyboards, vocals and tech) and teachers were asked to commit to one hour per week for at least one semester
2. Tuition was established at $5/week for each student, and they were asked to pay each week, not the whole semester in advance. Scholarships were made available so that no student would be left out
3. Accounting was to be done through the church, and each teacher was to receive a monthly check as an independent contractor. Most classes had at least 10 students the first semester
4. It was to be open to everyone, regardless of ability
5. The Sunday evening program was to begin with 10-minutes of a big-group worship time, then students were to be dismissed to their breakout classrooms
6. Sensitivity was given to other church events to avoid conflicts. The schedule was determined before the semester commenced, so families could make personal plans

Jamie Harvill

7. Each teacher was required to develop their own lessons and to submit a teaching plan. It was necessary that the teachers be endorsed by the pastoral staff, along with each having the necessary background checks and clearances to promote safety and security while working with children under the age of 18

8. At the conclusion of the semester, the number of students had grown beyond the 50 that started on the first week

9. Plans were made to expand classes when the second semester started

10. When implementing Worship Foundry at the second church, *Fender Musical Instruments* provided electric and acoustic guitars, basses, amps, and accessories for the students to use during the teaching sessions at the church

During the time that *Worship Foundry* operated, it was an incredible success. What a joy it was to see this dream realized. I look forward to helping other churches create a unique training opportunity like this.

In Conclusion

It wasn't perfect, but *Worship Foundry* proved that a comprehensive worship and music program could be launched and maintained in a small or large church. There are areas that will need to be customized for churches, most likely in the way of funding and payout for teachers. I chose to let students pay their tuition fees weekly, which was more affordable for the families involved. Paying tuition created a *dual commitment* between the teacher and student. You may choose to offer a program free of charge with a volunteer teaching staff.

Either way, the important thing is to raise up, to form a new generation of worship singers, musicians and technicians to one day move into the adult program, or even into full-time ministry. The apprentice form of training can prove to be an effective method in equipping young people in the church, especially in the area of music and worship.

Even if the Lord tarries, people are still going to be gathering each week in churches or living rooms to praise God, a hundred years—even a thousand years from now. They, too, will require strong leadership. Therefore, it is the responsibility of each successive generation to train up

Worship Foundry

the next generation of Christ-followers to serve the Body of Christ. This is the reason I wrote this book.

Though musical styles come and go—and technologies continue to evolve—the need for strong, undaunted, God-fearing worship leaders will remain one of the most important human ingredients in a healthy, growing church. I hope that the seeds sown in these pages will reap a bountiful harvest in the hearts of Godly leaders, who place the glory of God and service to others over personal gain.

I pray that your sincere goal as a worship leader is to forego fashion, the opinions of others—and the human tendency to take the easy route— but rather to seek the Lord's approval; to become a living sacrifice, fully pleasing to the Lord. At your journey's end, may you hear the Savior say, "Well done, my good and faithful servant!"

Jamie Harvill is available for speaking engagements, *Worship Foundry* training opportunities, and to lead worship for churches, conferences, organizations and groups. He is also available as a consultant. Please contact Jamie through his website: www.jamieharvill.com

RESOURCES

__Books__

Maxwell, John. *The 21 Irrefutable Laws of Leadership*. Revised & Updated Edition. Nashville: Thomas Nelson, 2007.

Saxena, Dr. P.K. *Principles of Management: A Modern Approach*. First Edition. Global India Publications Pvt. Ltd., 2009.

The Good News Translation of the Bible. 2nd Edition. Grand Rapids, MI: Zondervan Publishing Company, 2001.

The Merriam-Webster Dictionary. Encyclopedia Britannica. Revised Edition, 2004.

Backus, Truman J. *"The Dawn of the English Drama"* from *The Outlines of Literature: English and America*. New York: Sheldon and Company, 1897, 80-84.

Stevenson, Dr. Ann. *Dance! [God's Holy Purpose]*. Dance!Destiny Image, 2007.

Dickens, Charles. *David Copperfield*. Mineola, NY: Dover Publications, 2005.

The Holy Bible: New King James Version (NKJV). Nashville: Thomas Nelson, 2005.

Allen, Ronald B. *The Wonder of Worship*. Nashville: Word Publishing, 2000, 21-23, 179.

Spurgeon, Charles H. *"The Blessing of Worship."* The Metropolitan Tabernacle Pulpit, vol. 41.

Shelly, Rubel. *In Search of Wonder: A Call to Worship Renewal*, Lynn Anderson,ed. Brentwood,TN:Howard Books, 1995, 77.

Gaddy, C. Welton. *The Gift of Worship*. Nashville: Broadman Press, 1992.

The ESV Study Bible, First Edition. Wheaton, IL: Crossway, 2008.

Warren, Rick *The Purpose Driven Church*. Grand Rapids, MI: Zondervan Publishing House,1995.

Malphurs, Aubrey. *Developing a Vision for Ministry in the 21st century*. Grand Rapids, MI: Baker Books, 1999.

Barna, George. *Habits of Highly Effective Churches*. Ventura, CA: Regal Books, 1999.

Rainer, Thom. *High Expectations: The Remarkable Secret to Keeping People in Your Church*. Nashville: Broadman & Holman Publishers, 1999.

Wesley, John. *Explanatory Notes Upon the Old Testament*. Print Editions. Gale ECCO, 2010.

Brown, Jake. *Behind The Boards: The Making of Rock 'n' Roll's Greatest Records Revealed*. Milwaukee, WI: Hal Leonard Books, 2012, 359.

Articles/ Papers

Schulman, Dr. Matthew R., MD. "Beauty Defined" Healthy Aging Magazine. Digital Edition. (September 29, 2008).

Baumgartner, Jeffery Paul. "Characteristics of Highly Creative People." The Creativity Post (January 20, 2013).

Fant, Gene C., Jr. "On Hiring: Micromanagers and Administrator Types." The Chronicle of Higher Education (October 21, 2010).

Drake, Sir Frances. "Disturb Us, O Lord." Church Edge Blog (Nov. 1, 2007).

Sims, Dale B. "The Effect of Technology on Christianity: Blessing or Curse?" Dallas Baptist University.

Geirland, John. "Go With the Flow," Wired Magazine, Condé Nast Publications Inc., Wired Digital, Inc.

Kauflin, Bob "A Brief History of Congregational Song." Liturgies, Sonreign Media, Inc.

Murrow, David. "Why Men Have Stopped Singing In Church." A Few Grown Men, (http://www.patheos.com/blogs/afewgrownmen/).

Shaw, Tommy. "Tommy Shaw's Audience Rules" Kick Acts Magazine (October 8, 2010).

Albrecht, Leann. "The Fine Line of Fashion – Sensuous or Virtuous." www.leannalbrecht.com (February, 2011).

DVD/Video

Jackson, Tom, *"All Roads Lead to the Stage."* DVD Series, Tom Jackson's On Stage Success.

Taylor, James. *"Live Performance,"* Carnegie Hall, 9of9 (http://www.youtube.com/watchfeature=player_embedded&v=LE7e7mZvcbQ)

Yarrow, Peter. *"Peter, Paul & Mary: 25th Anniversary Concert DVD."* Shout Factory!, 2011.

Winfrey, Oprah, from an interview with Chris Witherspoon for NBC's Today Show. (http://www.today.com/video/today/52675209#52675209) August 5, 2013.

Internet

www.druckerinstitute.com
www.warrenbennis.com
www.purposequest.com
www.traditioninaction.org
www.thefreedictionary.com
www.saddleback.com
www.ccli.com
www.christiancopyrightsolutions.com
http://kidsareworthit.com/Barbara_s_Biography.html

Lightning Source UK Ltd.
Milton Keynes UK
UKOW03f1815080414

229626UK00001B/79/P